T0300246

Media Relations Measurement

Media
Relations
Measurement

Determining the Value of PR to Your Company's Success

Dr RALF LEINEMANN and
ELENA BAIKALTSEVA

Routledge
Taylor & Francis Group

LONDON AND NEW YORK

First published 2004 by Gower Publishing

Published 2016 by Routledge
2 Park Square, Milton Park, Abingdon, Oxon OX14 4RN
711 Third Avenue, New York, NY 10017, USA

Routledge is an imprint of the Taylor & Francis Group, an informa business

British Library Cataloguing in Publication Data
Leinemann, Ralf
Media relations measurement : determining the value of PR
to your company's success
1. Public relations - Evaluation
I. Title II. Baikaltseva, Elena
659.2
ISBN 0 566 08650 6

Library of Congress Cataloging-in-Publication Data
Leinemann, Ralf.
Media relations measurement : determining the value of PR to your company's success
/by Ralf Leinemann and Elena Baikaltseva
    p. cm.
Includes bibliographical references and index.
ISBN: 0-566-08650-6
1. Public relations--Evaluation. 2. Mass media and business. 3. Industrial management.
I. Baikaltseva, Elena. II. Title.

HD59.L45 2004
659.2'072--dc22

                                                            2004014042

ISBN 9780566086502 (hbk)

Contents

List of figures

Foreword

SANDRA MACLEOD

CHIEF EXECUTIVE, ECHO RESEARCH

Increasingly, communicators are being called upon to demonstrate the value and contribution of their activities to organisational success. As with all other management functions, it is becoming more and more the case that the very remit and appreciation of PR is dependent upon its measurement.

So, despite the old-fashioned traditionalists who have always claimed that 'PR is a black art that cannot be measured', it is not surprising to note the growing number of books on communications and measurement featuring PR evaluation. Produced in the main by academia and researchers, there is a noticeable silence from communicators on the front line, dealing with this issue on a day-to-day basis. *Media Relations Measurement: Determining the value of PR to your company's success* co-authored by Dr Ralf Leinemann and Elena Baikaltseva provides a meaningful and welcome contribution to this debate.

Based on their own real-life experiences and challenges within leading global companies and drawing on actual 'best practice' applications – not just theory – this book is a 'must read' for in-house communicators and for all aspiring PR executives and managers. Peppered with illustrations from leading researchers, PR agencies and their own 'world class' corporate models, there is something here for everyone who is committed to proving and adding value to their PR operation and management.

Realistic and straightforward, the authors have focused deliberately and specifically on media relations measurement alone, notably from a marketing communications angle, rather than tackling all aspects that may fall within the public relations umbrella, such as public affairs or issues management. Having said that, many of their forms and suggestions will be applicable to activities beyond product promotion.

Useful insights are provided on internal considerations, measuring a PR agency and contributing to Balanced Scorecards. The authors have also produced a quick reference guide to the pros and cons of various measurement approaches.

Very practical, down to earth, and filled with useful tips, forms and examples, this book provides a no-nonsense guide to equip today's PR practitioner with some of the tools and approaches that can be – and should be – implemented immediately to embark on the journey that is PR measurement.

Sandra Macleod has more than twenty years' experience in communications and reputation analysis and evaluation. Her international career spans Canada, France and the UK, including PA Management Consultants. Author and lecturer across five continents, Sandra has contributed to books on professional accountability and corporate social responsibility. Sandra is the first international Trustee of the Institute of Public Relations (USA), a Fellow of the Institute of Public Relations (UK) and Editorial Advisor to the *Corporate Communications Journal*.

Preface

The term PR is interpreted differently from company to company. For some, it covers the entire public relations spectrum, for others it stands for press relations.

Throughout this book, we shall consider PR as standing for the press relations of a company. This means, we shall look not only into the relationships with the traditional print media, but we shall also look into the relationships with media such as TV and new online media.

This book is aimed not only at PR managers of larger corporations, but also at communication specialists of smaller or medium-sized companies. It may also be of interest to managers of communications departments who have developed into this role from a different educational background and who are now supposed to learn on the job.

Whatever your individual history is, now that you are responsible for PR you will encounter one significant challenge. You will realise very soon that you are not alone. Many of your colleagues in marketing or in management positions are always prepared to give you advice on PR. In fact, there are two areas of expertise almost every manager in your company considers they know as well as the specialists: HR and PR.

Sometimes, you will need to prove your added value – and from time to time try to change peoples' opinions about what is wrong and what is right in your company's PR strategy. Facts based on thorough media analysis are the ideal foundation for these discussions.

Over the last ten years PR has developed considerably and the role of PR has become more visible within companies. Therefore, the need to measure the role and the effectiveness of PR work against company goals and objectives has become more pressing for PR managers and specialists.

In many countries PR organisations were established to provide help and discussion forums for PR professionals. These bodies are very helpful institutions since they can monitor local impact on PR. We shall see several times throughout this book that demands on PR can be different from country to country. Cultural aspects play a role, but also historical developments and different media landscapes per country. Also, the shape of the local economy has an influence on PR requirements. These different demands could also have an impact on media analysis criteria and tools. Again, local PR associations could be a very useful source for special needs per country – not only for local firms, but also for foreign companies that want to expand their business into a new country.[1]

---

1   To identify your local PR association, you may want to consult with the International Public Relations Association (IPRA) at *www.ipra.org* or you can also find a very good list of local associations on the website of the British Institute of PR at *www.ipr.org.uk*.

It needs to be noted that in fact today we do not necessarily talk separately about PR or advertising or promotions anymore – we talk about branding. And every company is interested in having the maximum return on their investments as well as a valuable tool ready to measure the results as they build the brand. In this respect, PR must learn from other disciplines. For example, we know how to measure a campaign and we know how to measure return on investments in advertising. For PR, though, no standards have yet been set in stone.

What makes this book different from others in the market is the fact that it was not written by members of a PR agency, but by PR managers of organisations which are closely aligned with the company's business objectives.[2]

We believe, though, that there are good reasons for every organisation to work with an external PR agency, or more specifically in this case, research and evaluation (R&E) agencies. Unlike advertising, there is no common measurement model in place for PR; evaluation typically has to be tailored to the company, its needs and its objectives. The many examples from agencies referenced in this book already indicate that there are advantages to having support from external resources. If you do not consult with external resources there is always a danger in seeing everything through rose-tinted glasses rather than being genuinely objective. Outsourced PR consultancy can help here. However, it needs to be integrated into the business objectives of the organisation and adapted to practical use.

Organisations want to have a tool for measuring readily accessible, to tell them if their investment is justified – agencies tend to use their measurement scheme to justify their services to their client. It is a common understanding that PR evaluation became a fashionable topic in the 1990s since agencies had to justify their rates in challenging economic times. The fact is that the PR departments of organisations are now going through a similar process. PR departments also have the challenge of either achieving certain PR goals or complying with a defined return-on-investment goal.

Organisations have one goal in mind: they want their business to be successful. PR is one of the key tools towards helping them achieve this goal. Investment justification on the one hand and services justification on the other hand looks like a small and subtle difference, but, in reality this difference may have interesting consequences. For example, you must ask yourself the question, how much of your time is spent on measuring the impact of your work versus spending your time directly on the PR work itself?

Measuring your PR activities should not be self-serving. It should not distract you from getting your work done in the first place. So, you may not want to waste time creating beautiful reports that are so detailed that nobody will want to take the time to read them – nor will anybody be able to draw conclusions from them.

---

2   Every PR agency tends to have its own measurement scheme that they use with their clients. Sometimes, they are very basic. Often, however, they are very sophisticated – and from time to time they are considered to be too complicated, too academic or too theoretical by their clients. In a worst-case scenario they are of no practical use.

The idea of this book is not only to bring together classical theories and approaches for PR measurements, even though you will find references to classical PR rules, it is also to show real examples of how to work on a day-to-day basis and to introduce ideas that have been proven to deliver results in practice.

We hope that this book becomes a valuable reference tool for everyday use.

DR RALF LEINEMANN
ELENA BAIKALTSEVA

CHAPTER 1

Initial Brainstorming

The trouble with not having a goal is that you can spend your life
running up and down the field and never score.
Bill Copeland (born 1926)

The following situation is familiar to all of us. We approach the end of a financial quarter or the end of a fiscal year and face a results review. All we have is the press clipping that was either put together by our PR agency or by ourselves. It is an impressive pile of paper that we proudly present to our management. Often we are surprised by their reaction. Either they just weigh it, or they flip through it with their thumbs, or if they want to be very polite, they take it home with them and return it to you after a week or so without having wasted a second reading it. Still, you may get some approving comments about the size of the coverage. In other words: your results were measured by kilograms of printed paper.

Despite the approval do you still feel uncomfortable?

That's fine!

It looks like you now have the right book in your hands to help you move further into the comfort zone – and to add more value to your company in your role as PR manager.

WHY DO I WANT TO MEASURE PR? – PART 1

Hewlett-Packard became world famous during its start-up phase for a concept that was new at the time. It was called 'management by objectives' (MBO). The concept was based on the idea that employees were most motivated and delivered best results not only when they were measured against certain goals that had been defined in a top-down approach, but also when they were involved in defining the goals and objectives themselves.

Manager and employee agreed on certain objectives for a certain period, typically one year, and evaluated the results on a regular basis. The process ensured the definition of challenging as well as achievable goals since they were agreed upon by both parties. The process also ensured the commitment of both the manager as well as the employee.

The MBO process incorporates regular performance reviews, feedback mechanisms and ultimately a remuneration scheme that is closely linked to the performance of every individual.

The definition of objectives is comparatively straightforward for certain professions like manufacturing or sales. It becomes more complicated for other professions like marketing or communication related jobs like PR.

Regardless of the objectives you select, the important thing is that the results can be measured. Objectives without measurement schemes are useless. They do not help you to determine an employee's contribution to the company.

In PR, you typically end up either with soft measures like feedback from higher-level management or the satisfaction level of the product marketing organisation, or a very sophisticated measurement scheme is developed.

Measuring the results of employees' work is one reason for introducing PR measure-ment schemes. But there are other reasons too.

In every company PR is a cost centre. PR costs money, and the return on investment is not visible immediately. As a result, PR is typically one of the first items in the budget spreadsheet to be cut if the financial situation of the company requires it. In fact, the amount of money put into the PR industry has proven to be an early indicator for the economy as a whole of going strong or slowing down - very similar to the advertising business.

An article in the German *Handelsblatt* dated 9 July 2002 is a perfect example to support this statement. The article (*Unternehmens-PR kommt auf den Prüfstand*, by Jürgen Hoffmann) discusses the fact that corporate PR in many German companies was closely evaluated at the time. The soft economy has caused many PR budgets to be tighter than expected. In particular, Deutsche Telekom was looked at. The company's stock price had gone down from above $100 to only about $10. As a result, PR in particular, but also direct marketing and sponsoring were cut significantly. Only a few days later, the leading German newspapers announced a significant decrease, by up to 45 percent, in income brought through advertising. Again, the conclusion drawn was that the economy would slow down even further in the near future.

There are two obvious reasons why PR typically suffers first when times get tougher:

1. It is extremely easy to cut the PR budget.

2. Apparently there is no immediate impact on sales.

What is often overlooked is that while achieving short-term sales goals, a company with reduced PR resources typically damages its long-term visibility in the market. Unfortunately, companies listed at the stock exchange in particular feel under pressure to give higher priority to short-term shareholder values than to the long-term prosperity of the company.

We would argue that at times of budget cuts PR on average suffers substantially more than other cost centres. Even though this may be justified in many cases, often the decision is only taken due to a lack of understanding of what the actual impact of those cuts will be.

In order to gain a complete understanding of the implications of increasing or decreasing PR resources, it is imperative for every company's management to measure its PR results, because

You can only manage what you measure.

However, the measurement of PR should not be done for the sole purpose of justifying the existence of the PR department – even though there may be a good reason why the value of the PR department is questioned from time to time. After you have read this book carefully you will hopefully have gained more idea of what systems you want to implement in your company. And once you have implemented those processes and measures, you will be able to show your results and demonstrate the value PR brings to your company. Still, the question can be asked: what was the *incremental* value of your work above what the press would have written about your company anyway – without a PR department even existing. The answers to that question can be any of the below, or a combination thereof:

- PR has increased the volume of press coverage.

- PR has improved the tone of what is written.

- PR has ensured that content was covered that the company intended to be covered.

- PR has ensured that a negative topic was *not* covered (crisis communication, see Chapter 7).

- PR indeed had no impact. (If you ever have to admit this, you may want to consider a change in your career.)

So, it is indeed a valuable exercise at some point in time to separate the *added* value of the PR department from what we may want to call 'background noise'. In this context, the 'background noise' would be coverage (volume and tone) that appears in the press even without the active involvement of a PR department. For example, if you were the market leader in your specific field the media would hardly be able to avoid writing about you. Or, if you announced some spectacular business news like a major acquisition, an unexpected financial result or a significant customer win, again the press would most likely write about it, with or without your active involvement.

In reality, it is almost impossible to determine exactly this 'background noise'. Sometimes it may be possible to get some idea of its size by looking into your PR performance in countries where you do not actively do any PR – but even that approach may be faulty due to local influences that cannot be transferred to other countries. You may also have a closer look at what is written about you in quiet periods when you do not run any active PR campaigns.

Regardless of how you determine the 'background noise' or generic coverage, you should notice primarily two impacts of your active PR work. You should see a more positive tone in the coverage and you should see a higher volume – depending on your PR goals. Ultimately, the difference between your generated coverage and your generic coverage, that is, your calibrated coverage, would be the added value that you bring to your company, and the reason why the company wants to invest in you. Your capabilities to manage communication during a crisis, though, can be of much higher value to your company. We want to look into this aspect separately, though, since it is a very specific topic with very different measures.

Still, just trying to justify the existence of the PR department would be a very defensive approach to demonstrating the value of PR. Measuring PR is not just about defending the profession itself or defending and justifying budgets and jobs.

There are, of course, also business reasons for measuring PR. PR can be used as a competitive tool, it helps to define strategic programmes, it improves focus, provides feedback on the content and it allows continuous improvement. And, of course, it shows return on investments.

Using PR as a competitive tool requires you to stay in control and still outperform your competitors. The PR measurement will help you stay in control. This is, however, a contradiction of the famous statement by the popular racing driver Mario Andretti, who once said 'When you are still in control, you are not going fast enough'.

The results of PR are often only shared with senior management in order to create internal awareness of the PR activities or – even more so – visibility and recognition of individual PR managers. The typical procedure would then be to share positive PR results, while less good results are kept a secret. And often 'positive' is dependent on a very subjective opinion of an individual. The result would be recognition of the achievements and a lot of mutual back slapping.

Usually, there are no other consequences.

In this scenario nobody learns from the results, especially not from the negative ones. No corrective action will be taken and the same mistakes will then happen again with the next PR campaign. This behaviour is similar to that of a child who only shares positive results from school with his parents. Negative ones are ignored and/or hidden.

What a missed opportunity, when we know that you can always learn most from negative results.

A simple consequence is:

Measures only make sense when you are willing to learn from the results.

It should be noted here that it is comparatively easy to avoid this scenario by clearly separating the functional measurement from measuring individuals. For example, the performance of the PR manager may have been a very good one over a certain period in time – and it should show in his personal evaluation. Even so, the PR results may have been unsatisfactory. However, the cause for those results may have been beyond the PR manager's control.

In this context it is difficult to use the above comparison with the behaviour of a child. Children have a tendency to look for excuses as to why they did not achieve the expected results. Poor PR results should never be the reason for excuses, but should prompt a thorough investigation of the causes – which may not even be inside your company.

WHY DO I WANT TO MEASURE PR? – PART 2

Another approach to answering the above question would be to take a look at the generic value of PR to the corporation. PR is a window that your company consciously opens to communicate with the world outside. But, a window also allows people to look inside your company. True communication is never just a one-way street, but should be a dialogue and should add value to both parties involved.

In the case of a company's PR activities, one should not just try to get a message out, but also to learn from the experience and opinions of the media representatives. Journalists' feedback can be a very valuable source of information: not only to give direct feedback on your announcement, but also to provide generic comments on observed trends and potentially indirect feedback from your customers, the readers of the journalists' articles.

Just as the feedback of a single journalist during an interview is of interest to you, the accumulated feedback from the media should be of even greater interest to you. A proper media evaluation should provide you with exactly that: a survey of the opinions expressed in the media.

Surprisingly enough, many companies keep inbound and outbound communication strictly separate; PR is considered to be their outbound tool, while information is brought into the company through business intelligence, market intelligence or – if more closely linked to sales – business development teams. These companies decide to spend a significant amount of money on market research, industry analyst research, participation at conferences, trade reports, data mining, etc. But they also decide not to make use of a free information source.

You could argue that the feedback of a single journalist may be free. A proper media evaluation tailored specifically for your company, though, is expensive and can take up a significant portion of your overall PR budget (see also Chapter 2).

This is true. However, one can argue the point in a different way. Compare your media evaluation expense with other information gathering tools and the cost suddenly appears in a different light.

It is interesting to observe that companies are willing to spend a lot of money on awareness and preference studies or customer surveys but shy away from dedicating a proper budget to media evaluation. At a Harvard Debate[1] in London in October 2002, Ralf Leinemann argued that media evaluation may even save you money because it can often be a far less expensive way of getting access to information than other tools.

---

1   'Evaluation – Linking PR to corporate success' (17 October 2002), organised by Harvard Public Relations.

This may be an extreme standpoint, but, companies that do not coordinate business intelligence and media evaluation results miss an important point. Firstly, they disregard the opportunity to check their collected data for consistency. And secondly, they miss the opportunity to compare their customers' feedback with that of those people who influence their future opinions and attitudes – the journalists.

If media evaluation, however, is used as an extension to the results of business intelligence activities, it becomes an extremely powerful tool. All of a sudden it becomes a basis for decisions in the boardroom and has a direct impact on the results of the company and the bottom line. There was a strong consensus among the participants of the above mentioned Harvard Debate that media evaluation is a key tool to gaining respect in the boardroom.

HOW CAN PR BE MEASURED?

This simple question has kept generations of PR managers and communication specialists busy. A quick comparison with sports will show why it has proved to be such a challenge.

Disciplines that are measured in distance, time, height or weight are objective. Whoever is fastest in the 100 metres race wins the competition. But how about figure skating? Here the subjective impression left with a judge decides the outcome of the competition. And arguing about results seems to have become a standard procedure after every major competition nowadays.

The same is true in the industry.

For example, the results of a manufacturing plant can easily be measured. The number of items manufactured per given length of time tells you immediately what the organisation has achieved. And not only can the quantity be measured, but also the quality. Regular quality checks can immediately give you an idea about the number of defective parts or parts that deviate from the pre-defined norm.

A sales organisation can also be measured in a very straightforward way. The generated order volume is all that counts. High order numbers equal a good result. Low order numbers equal room for improvement.

Measurement problems already start when one tries to measure a marketing organisation. And it typically becomes an absolute nightmare when trying to measure communication in general or PR in particular. You may have beautiful structures and processes in place like:

1.   A well defined *data source*, typically your press clippings, leading to

2.   Your well-structured *database* containing any important information on journalists, publications, and so on. Your database would be the foundation for

3.   Any *analytical research*, for example, on trends and ultimately leading to

4.   Your media analysis *reports*.

Still, you can be very flexible when defining your data source, determining the content of your database, identifying the focus of your research and deciding on the content of your reports. In other words: it is completely up to you to decide on your measurement process and the content. This can in fact be very dangerous, since you may go for goals that are far too easily attainable – or, you cannot possibly achieve. Goals should be ambitious, no challenge is no value added. But, at the same time, they should be realistic.

As a result, authors writing books on PR very often try to avoid the subject of evaluation. They either only dedicate a short appendix to the topic, they do not cover it at all, or they brush over it with generic comments like 'it is practically impossible to show the effectiveness of PR in detail in an analytical or economical way'.[2]

DEFINING GOALS

This book is about measuring PR, but, before we actually do so, we need to ask some more basic questions. What do we want to measure against? What do we want to compare? What were the goals we wanted to achieve in the first place? Or, in other words:

No objectives - no measures.

To be precise, setting goals and carrying out the evaluation are only two parts of a larger process that can be described as the overall communication model. Before you set goals, you obviously want to know what your current situation is. And after you have completed your PR activity, you probably want to do another situation analysis to define your future steps. And between the planning phase and the evaluation, you have an execution phase.

The entire process can be considered a circle that you should work through either per project or, maybe on an annual basis:

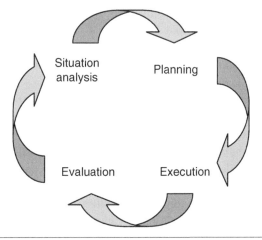

Figure 1.1 The PR process

---

2 This statement is taken from *30 Minuten für erfolgreiche Presse-und Öffentlichkeitarbeit*, by Jens Ferber, Gabal Verlag, 2000.

In some literature you may also find that the cycle consists of five phases. In that case the planning phase is split into two separate steps. The first one would be the definition of the goals as derived from the situation analysis, and the actual planning or definition of the strategy would be another step.

Aristotle's famous phrase 'The beginning is half of the total' takes on an interesting meaning in this context, since you will have to ask yourself for every project, where your beginning actually is. It is obviously not in the planning phase of your new PR project, but already exists in the evaluation of the preceding activity.

PR goals can be very different. They can range from creating awareness for the company as a whole all the way to introducing a product. Or the goal is simply to create mind share with the journalists or to position a company spokesperson as an industry leader in the media. The objective could be to have numerous short articles across many publications or just a single favourable article in a pre-defined leading business magazine.

In the (special) case of crisis management, the objectives are typically exactly the opposite of normal PR. For example, getting no coverage on a product flaw would be much more desirable than reading in bold letters on the first page of the most influential newspaper that your company made a mistake.

So, depending on the objectives of the PR activities or a specific PR campaign, not only could the tactics be very different, but also, the measures used to claim success or failure could be different as well.

Even though goals can be very different, they all need to have certain attributes. According to Peter F. Drucker[3] who works on management by objectives, goals need to be **s**pecific, **m**easurable, **a**chievable, **r**elevant and **t**imely – or SMART. This is in fact a very good summary of the attributes of a PR goal. We will see later in chapter 3 that this basic requirement actually applies to several levels at which you can measure your PR results. We shall also see several times that goals can be subjective – similar to the above figure skating example. This is not a contradiction! PR is not an exact science. Not everything can be put into objective numbers and it is not a crime to have subjective parameters in your measurement system. You just need to be aware of the fact that they are!

The most basic goal is typically considered to get a good article in a defined publication – or in the case of a press conference addressing multiple journalists, a certain number of good articles.

But already this basic example shows the problem of measuring PR. What is a *good* article? Asking two colleagues in the company to define a good article will probably result in three different definitions.

The technician would probably have difficulties in understanding why the business press was targeted and not a technical publication. He would be delighted to see all the bells and whistles of the product being highlighted, together with a nice product shot.

---

3   Peter F. Drucker is a noted organisation development guru, whose work gained recognition in 1954 with
    the publication of his book, *The Practice of Management*.

The spokesperson who gave the interview to the journalist would like a copy of the article immediately just because he is quoted in it - and he would fall in love with the journalist if he even placed a photo of him next to the article. He would probably copy and enlarge the article and hang it up on the wall next to his desk in the office, in addition to showing it to friends and family.

Members of the company board will think more strategically. They would pay attention to the fact that the company is positioned properly or to whether the article addresses key messages and/or strategic directions of the company.

And so on, and so on …

This simple example probably shows that just having a *good* article as a result of a press interview is not a proper objective – unless you think that any coverage is good coverage, that the important part is to get a mention, regardless of whether it is positive or negative.

It is much better to decide in advance what you would like the article to achieve for the business and how you would like the article to look in the press. You may want to think in advance what you would like to see in the headline. Not only does this provide a strong guidance for the company spokesperson or for the writer of the press release, but this also allows you to compare the actual result with your intentions.

BASIC MEASURE

The most basic measure of a PR activity is extremely simple. It is to see if an article has been written at all after some PR activity.

You may want to argue that this is so basic that it should go without saying and should not really be a measure. Well, this is only true if you believe that every interview or any press release distribution automatically results in coverage. If you really think this, it is strongly recommended that you wake up and face the realities of PR.

An average journalist today probably receives more unsolicited material for publication than he actually has space for in his magazine. The value of PR is to present your own story in such a way that the journalist cannot avoid it and is convinced that it is to the benefit of his readers (not to his own, and definitely not to yours!). He will feel compelled to cover it while dropping nine other stories.

If you indeed believed that distributing a press release generates nice articles, you have probably never considered PR to be a serious profession – unfortunately, a common problem!

It should be understood that a press release posted through a business wire service will catch a journalist's attention for as long as it takes him to chase a fly away from a piece of paper on his desk.

It is the job of the PR professionals to ensure that this does not happen. It is the job of the PR professionals to ensure that their own message stands out from the others. It is the job of the PR professionals to ensure that your own story is not just part of the background noise …

PR is the art of tailoring content for a well-defined target audience.

Just as a sales representative should know the language of his customer, a PR manager should know the language of his *customers*, the media.

So, a first success can be celebrated when an article has been published as the result of a press release distribution, a press conference or a targeted one-to-one interview – and as the result of a good relationship with the media. (We will cover the relationship aspect of PR in a separate section in this book.)

It should be common practice in a PR department to collect press clippings and keep them for future reference. It will be useful to compare the article with future articles by the same author and, for example, see his attitude towards your company change – ideally, of course, in a positive way.

It would also be extremely interesting to see if the article has been picked up by the target audience you wanted it to reach – your customers, your shareholders, your business partners. A very positive sign would be to see the article being referenced by a potential new customer. In that case you may even be able to claim an immediate positive impact on your company's sales figures.

But it should be understood that this closed loop will always be the exception. In general it is much more likely that the true impact of the generated article will be hidden, probably forever.

Nevertheless, the pure quantitative data about the number of articles generated by the company's PR team should be considered a first measure. In retrospect, a goal could have been to generate a certain number of articles as a result of a press conference.

Even though the number of articles is a measurable item – and it should be measured – it does not tell me if my PR activity was successful!

There are several reasons why:

- I do not know anything yet about the tone of the article. Was the coverage positive or was your new product considered to be too expensive, the company strategy assumed to be leading in the wrong direction, or was your spokesperson misunderstood?

- Was the article only a short note in the middle of the publication or a leading article on the front page?

- Was the article accompanied by a picture or other graphical materials?

- Did the article lead with a strong headline?

- Did the author cover your story exclusively in the article, or did he integrate it into a feature article?

And one of the most basic questions has not even been asked yet …

HOW DO YOU COMPARE WITH THE COMPETITION?

Let us take a quick step back. Why are we doing PR in the first place? Is this again one of these things that should go without saying? Well, maybe – maybe not! The fact that many PR measures today do not address this basic point shows us that this definitely does not go without saying.

The obvious goal of PR is to create public awareness of your company, your products and your services. You do PR because you are working in a competitive landscape. There are other companies out there which would be more than happy to take business away from you - just like you would love to take it from them. So, your goal must not be simply to be visible, but to be better than your competitors.

Be better than your competitor.

This basic statement holds true for manufacturing, for sales, for finance or for any function in your company. It also holds true for PR.

So, although it is gratifying to see ten glowing articles in the press after a press conference, their true value, however, depends significantly on what your competitors have been doing at the same time. Have they been quiet or have they even suffered from negative press? In that case your ten articles could be worth pure gold.

However, if they have managed to get 100 excellent articles into the media at the same time they have overshadowed you completely. In that case all your efforts may not have paid off at all and your return on investment was significantly less than at first appeared.

A golden rule, therefore, should be to:

Always compare your PR performance with the competition.

Money spent on an agency providing a clipping service to collect your own articles would be a waste. This type of service would keep you blinkered – and you may celebrate success at a time when the alarm bells should in fact be ringing.

In his book *Grundwissen Öffentlichkeitsarbeit* (2002), Werner Faulstich describes the collection of clippings as a naïve approach to media analysis. He claims that 'the plain collection and the more or less intuitive rating of press clippings based on gut feeling … only serves vanity and self-sufficiency'.

CHAPTER 2

Basic Tools and Processes

Without some goal and some efforts to reach it, no man can live.
Fyodor Dostoevsky (1821–81)

LET'S GET SOME STRUCTURE INTO MEASUREMENTS

We have not pinned down any definite structure yet, but we have talked about measuring the result of an interview and measuring the result of a press conference. It should be understood, though, that a press conference or an interview are just two activities out of a whole arsenal of things you can choose from in PR. Tactical implementations for executing PR projects can be very different depending on your specific needs and goals. They require different measurement schemes and criteria. In general, we can differentiate between two measurements: we either want to measure the results of a specific campaign or we want to measure the results of PR generically. In this book, we want to take a more detailed look at five different aspects of PR measurement:

1.   PR project I: An individual interview.

2.   PR project II: A press conference.

3.   PR project III: A generic PR campaign.

4.   Generic long-term PR results.

5.   A PR crisis situation.

We have already learned that we are able to measure the coverage resulting from a PR campaign by

*   Quantity, and
*   Quality.

Prominence is often considered a third basic measurement criterion. We shall come back to that later.

A very basic quantitative measure would be the number of generated articles, while a typical qualitative measure would be the tone of an article. This is often also referred to as the rating of an article or the favourability.

We can also differentiate between *internal* and *external* results. Internal measures would be, for example, the effectiveness of spokespeople or response times to media enquiries, an external measure would be if the intended message was covered in the generated coverage.

With all of the above, it should be understood that PR measures could also be different depending on the target audience of the PR campaign. This is true for:

- Ultimate targets (customers, business partners, other influencers, for example, analysts).

- The customers (consumers, businesses, end-users).

The measures depend on the media you select to reach your target audience:

- The type of media (TV, radio, paper press, on-line publications).

- The focus of the media (for example trade, business press, daily newspapers).

Finally, we examine the true soft measures of PR. The 'R' in PR stands for relations. So, an interesting question is also to see how to measure relationships. In several chapters in this book we shall have a look into how to measure relationships with the press.

In general, we may want to consider measurements on five different levels (see also Chapter 3):

1. Internal Level
    Example: Number of interviews facilitated per given period of time.

2. Tactical or Output Level
    Example: Attendance at a press conference.

3. Relationship Level
    Example: Journalists allow proofreading before publishing.

4. Coverage Level
    Example: Intended company message versus message in coverage.

5. Outcome Level
    Example: Public opinion or preference.

It should be obvious from the above, but we still want to stress the fact here that all of the above measures the success of PR activities. Measuring *the individuals* executing the PR work is only loosely connected to the measurements we discuss in this book. This should become very clear in the next chapter, where we discuss business fundamentals. Business fundamentals describe parameters that are crucial for a business. They do not describe the performance of the people who contribute to achieving the goals defined in business fundamentals.

For example, it may be crucial for the business to create visibility in the media through achieving product press awards in reviews (see Appendix C). Thus, a business fundamental measuring the number and quality of achieved product press awards is introduced. A person or team in the organisation is charged with achieving those goals. After some time it becomes apparent that they do not achieve satisfactory results against the defined business fundamental. Does that mean that they have done a bad job? Maybe – maybe not. It could be that they have indeed set up a poor process or they have executed a good process in a poor way. However, it could also be that their products objectively do not match those of the competition. In that case, they cannot be blamed for a poor individual performance. *But*, in that case those who set unrealistic goals must be blamed for a poor performance!

DEFINING GOALS – BUSINESS FUNDAMENTALS

Your company or your company entity usually has a business plan. On the one hand, this business plan could be a very formal document that has been developed using standard planning processes like for example a ten-step-business planning process, from customer analysis to the first year's plan. On the other hand, it could be just an idea in your company's managing director or general manager's head. Either way, all employees of the company should be fully aware of the direction of the company and the defined goals – and all resources in the company should comply with the direction of the company.

The business plan should break down into business fundamentals that are reviewed on a regular basis, for example a review could be done every quarter. (In many companies this is in fact not necessarily done as part of the business planning process itself, but via a more tactical planning process like, for example, a Hoshin Plan.[1]) Defining business fundamentals is not an easy task. Basically, the business fundamentals should provide a snapshot of how the company is doing on its journey towards the defined goals.

A typical approach is to derive functional plans from the business plan. These may include: a sales plan including quotas; a marketing plan; a manufacturing plan and a communication plan. All these plans should have measurable goals, depending on the size and the history of the company and on its ambition. These range from maybe just one or two breakthrough goals per year all the way to a very sophisticated set of criteria to measure achievements over time.[2]

The objective of business fundamentals is to provide a quick overview, or a management summary of the status quo. They must be kept short and simple. Ideally, they show on a single page how the various entities of the company are doing. So, sales may only have a single line item: quota performance. Manufacturing may have two or three line items, one on volume, one on product quality and one on cost.

---

1   Some people refer to Hoshin planning as a 'philosophy of management'. Hoshin planning or 'Hoshin Kanri' is a combination of a Japanese development and management approach introduced first in the USA, including MBO (Management By Objectives) and the Plan-Do-Check-Act improvement cycle.

2   Breakthrough goals are also often referred to as Key Success Factors (KSAs) or Key Results Areas (KRAs).

HOW ABOUT PR?

Depending on the importance of PR for the company, PR may not be represented at all – which is not really recommended – or it appears as just a one line item.

This one line item could be very different from company to company, for example it would be dependent on the market share of the company, the history of the company or the ambition of the company. It should be noted here that business fundamentals should not be set in stone for the next twenty years. In fact, business fundamentals themselves should be subject to reviews typically every one to two years.

Now, let us discuss several scenarios and see how to apply PR measures to business fundamentals. We will introduce here three scenarios and three measures:

1. *Quantitative.* Your company has been in business for many years. You normally experience a reasonable press coverage compared to the competition. New products or services you are planning to introduce next year will allow your company for the first time in history to stand up against the competition. Your business fundamental until now was modest. You were satisfied when the media gave you a fair share of voice compared to other vendors. In fact, you measured yourself against the coverage of the market leader:

    If you got 25 per cent of the market leader's coverage, you considered yourself to be in good shape, or in 'green' shape.

    If you experienced 15-25 per cent of the market leader's press coverage, you started to raise an attention flag, or you considered yourself in 'yellow'.

    And if you experienced less than 15 per cent of the market leader's coverage, you raised the 'red' flag causing corrective actions.

    For three of the last four quarters, you have proved to be in good (green) shape, only for one quarter you moved briefly into the yellow state.

    It is obvious that the current business fundamental will no longer be sufficient next year. You want to increase your 'share of ink'. You want to see a stronger impact, more bold statements in the press than before.

    At the same time, PR is recognised to be of higher value to the company than before. Working with the media is considered to become more strategic to the company. As a result, you want to provide your executives with a more detailed picture of what happens in PR. Consequently, you are now dealing with two business fundamentals instead of just one.

    Your new business fundamentals may now look like this:

    • If you grow your share of media voice by four percentage points or more per quarter, you are in green.

        If you only grow between one and four percentage points per quarter, you are in yellow.

        If you only grow by one percentage point or less, you are in red.

- You may want to start counting press enquiries as a measure for the interest your company stimulates in the industry. Since you have not measured this before, you should not measure absolute values, but trends such as growth rates.

You have probably noticed that both new measures are no longer measures of absolute values such as number of articles or favourability rating, but relative growth rates. Using growth rates is highly recommended in a dynamic environment. It is necessary, however, to always measure them on the same basis. So, for example, you cannot change the number of evaluated publications over time without impacting your statistics. Neither should you replace individual titles by others.

This statement is obvious, but often in reality causes issues, since the media landscape is a dynamic one. Publications disappear from the market and new ones are created. Any such changes need to be documented very clearly in order to avoid misinterpretation of your data.

You can eliminate this issue by measuring articles per publication over time. But, as you will see in Chapter 6, this will cause new challenges you need to pay attention to.

2. *Qualitative.* Your company has just suffered from a significant crisis that resulted in a negative impact on the image of your brand. In this scenario, the focus in your PR work over the next 12 months or so should not be to generate volume, but be driven by quality. For example, you should have a close look into the favourability or the tone of the articles written about your company.

    So, you may want to define a business fundamental like:

    Green: Ratio of positive/neutral articles against total number of articles grows by 10 per cent or more per quarter.

    Yellow: Ratio of positive/neutral articles against total number of articles grows by 3-10 per cent per quarter.

    Red: ratio of positive/neutral articles against total number of articles grows by less than 3 per cent per quarter.

Once you are back to normal, you may want to change your measure back to what you had before the crisis.

3. *Internal.* You notice that articles based on interviews with your executives have a significantly stronger impact than those based on generic press releases. As a result, you want selected executives to spend more time with the press.

    In this case you may want to introduce an internal measure as a business fundamental like this:

    Green: 20 or more interviews with the press are facilitated per quarter.

    Yellow: 10-20 interviews are facilitated.

    Red: Less than 10 interviews are facilitated.

Be aware that with a measure like this you need to be able to interpret the results properly afterwards. Not achieving your goals could have been due to various reasons:

- Your executives are not committed to PR. (Maybe their job descriptions demand them to focus on other topics.)

- You have set unrealistically high goals.

- The intention to set up an interview cannot replace lack of news.

- If your responsibility spans across countries, you may have tried to promote spokespeople with the incorrect language skills in certain countries.

- You have not worked out talking points together with your spokesperson or did not brief the spokesperson accordingly (normally valid for larger corporations).

If you are fortunate enough to have three business fundamentals in your company, this either shows that your company puts a very strong focus on PR – or it shows that there are too many business fundamentals defined overall.

In an ideal world of being represented with three business fundamentals, it should be good practice to define one quantitative and one qualitative measure, and an internal measure in addition.

An internal measure might be the number of facilitated interviews as shown above. It may also be something that stimulates internal recognition or incentives. For example, if your entity is responsible for a certain region, you may want to identify a fundamental like 'to be the region with the best PR results' – whatever the criteria may then be in detail.

It should be noted that a measure like this one is bound to stimulate internal competition, and whether this is healthy or destructive depends significantly on the company culture.

It should also be noted that internal measures in a business fundamentals table could be considered a luxury. They do not necessarily measure the success of the business directly. So, in theory, they should not be in a business fundamentals table in the first place. However, they can be considered to be a measure that acts as an early warning system for the organisation.

For example, if you define the number of press interviews with your executives to be a business fundamental, then a low value could hint that PR is of low priority on your executives' agendas. And this, in return, means that one of your most valuable PR resources are of limited availability only, potentially resulting in decreasing visibility of your company in the media.

Some typical business fundamentals are shown overleaf:

Measure 1 – Quantitative:

 More than 80% of positive/neutral coverage of competitor A

 50–80% of positive/neutral coverage of competitor A

 Less than 50% of positive/neutral coverage of competitor A

Measure 2 – Qualitative:

 More than 90% of articles are neutral or positive

 70–90% of articles are neutral or positive

 Less than 70% of articles are neutral or positive

Measure 3 – Internal:

 In more than 95% of the cases we responded to a journalist's enquiry within his given deadline.

 In 80–95% of the cases we responded to a journalist's enquiry within his given deadline.

 In less than 80% of the cases we responded to a journalist's enquiry within his given deadline.

The results of one business year could then look as follows:

	Quarter 1	*Quarter 2*	*Quarter 3*	*Quarter 4*
Measure 1	Red	Red	Yellow	Green
Measure 2	Yellow	Yellow	Yellow	Green
Measure 3	Red	Yellow	Green	Green

At first glance, this table requires some interpretation.

It could be, for example, that the company had recognised at the beginning of the year that it was not very responsive to the media's requests for information. This could also have been an explanation for the poor representation in the media's coverage. Maybe as a result a goal has been defined to react faster to enquiries. As the table shows, the company has improved significantly throughout the year, and as a result, not only did the coverage increase (with a latency that had to be expected), but also the quality of the written articles improved over time.

It is to be noted that, this example shows that at the end of the year, all goals were achieved. However, it needs a watchful eye to be kept to see if everything stays in green during the following quarters. Still, everything being in green should trigger the idea of going for more ambitious goals in the following year.

Be ambitious, but do not be unrealistic!

Example: Business fundamentals

Hewlett-Packard was very successful with the use of business fundamentals as described in this chapter. For example, in one of the HP organisations, two business fundamentals for PR per country in the EMEA (Europe, Middle-East, Africa) region were introduced a few years ago. One measured the amount of press coverage and a second one measured the tone in the articles as compared to the five most relevant competitors.

The results were tracked on a monthly basis. It was immediately noticed that some countries did better than others. This was partly due to different competitive landscapes in those countries and partly due to other factors.

The media analysis showed what countries had to focus on in order to improve their performance. Stronger focus, sharing best practices from other countries and other actions resulted in significant performance increases within a year or even less. In one country HP advanced from fourth position to second, in one even from fourth to first. And, in two countries HP climbed from fifth to second and after a year even competed for the top spot as being the most visible company and the company with the best favourability rating in the media.

A final comment in this chapter is dedicated to the focus of business fundamentals. Until now, we have only looked at fairly generic examples. For small or medium-sized companies their use should be straightforward. Larger corporations, however, often have the need to focus.

Consider companies like General Electric, Sony, Hewlett-Packard or Samsung, all with very broad product portfolios. Often, they also address a wide range of customers from consumers to businesses. A plain business fundamental like 'number of generated articles' could be meaningless to such a company, since it may not reflect the communication objectives. If your objective is to grow in a certain product category or a certain customer segment, then your measures should reflect that objective. So, the generic fundamental should be changed, for example, to 'number of generated articles for product X' or 'number of generated articles in a defined media segment'.

A focused business fundamental would immediately align PR measurements with the business objectives. One should, however, also be aware of the negative aspects of such an approach: the overall PR performance would become invisible – at least in the business fundamentals. The advantages of a focused metrics, however, significantly outweigh the disadvantages.

We can look look at this in more detail in the following example: we assume that you are working in an industry that is undergoing significant changes due to technology advances. Typical examples are moves to digital technology in the music industry (records to CDs), the film industry (VHS to DVDs) and the move to digital photography. If you have been a major player before the technology revolution, you want to make a move into the new technologies at some point in time. This move may be the most important move in the history of your company – and it may be crucial for the destiny of the overall corporation. At a time like this you want to be sure that your PR activities are focusing clearly on supporting the company's strategy. In a case like this you may want to measure only the generated coverage that refers to your company's move. 'Generic' articles covering your traditional business should not be included in your business fundamentals. It would not only portray the wrong picture of your achievements, but in this specific case it would even count distracting articles as positive results in the business fundamentals. Another negative aspect would be the attitude and behaviour of the PR managers, who would be encouraged to continue to work in their comfort zone, with the old technology.

DEFINING GOALS – MARKETING PLAN, COMMUNICATION PLAN, AND PR PLAN

Once a business plan is defined in your company, the foundation is laid. All other planning should refer back to this 'constitution'.

The natural next step towards defining PR goals is typically looking into the marketing plan. It defines strategic objectives, breakthrough issues and goals, tactical processes and forthcoming milestones.

In some rare cases, however, you may see that a PR plan comes first (here PR stands for the more generic public relations). That means in some cases PR objectives may influence marketing strategies. Areas where this can be seen from time to time are commodity businesses or the banking sector.

The marketing plan, in return, should be the basis for a communication plan. In some companies the communication plan is also referred to as a marcom (marketing communication) plan. This plan should summarise and coordinate all inbound and outbound communication into various target audiences, for example:

- employees, sales force
- channel partners
- business partners
- media representatives
- security analysts
- industry analysts and other influencers
- shareholders
- customers, consumers, end-users.

It should be noted that in some companies the PR plan is integrated into this marcom plan, in some companies it is treated separately. Both approaches have advantages and disadvantages.

An advantage of working across multiple marcom mix elements is to achieve close integration of your messages across various target audiences. Also, it allows you to define consistent goals across all marcom mix elements such as advertising, PR, direct marketing and so on. One interesting aspect becomes apparent when working across all communication disciplines: PR is typically the one discipline that is most easily measured by neutral resources, that is external agencies. An external PR clipping service or a more sophisticated PR evaluation service can provide feedback on the PR performance while other disciplines are often measured only from within the company – like, for example, in direct marketing where the return rate of mailings is a typical criteria for success. (It should be noted, however, that the return on investment of direct marketing campaigns can be more easily obtained, for example, when executing a well-defined campaign through a call centre.)

In practice, the close integration sometimes results in messages not being tailored to the needs of the individual audiences. This would mean, for example, that journalists are addressed as if they were customers and they were being sold to. In a worst-case scenario, they would even share the same collateral with other communities. A journalist would then 'enjoy' receiving product brochures or data sheets, or an industry analyst would have the 'pleasure' of getting press releases. In smaller companies with limited staff this is a common mistake.

Here once again we need to understand clearly that journalists are not the target audience of the company or enterprise. At the end of the day, they are not the ones who buy our products. But they help us to sell, like a middleman. So, it is the task of a PR manager to ensure that information given to the press is positioned as 'how to sell' rather than a sales presentation itself. In fact, our messages are only attractive to journalists when we also help them to 'sell' – to attract their readers (that is, our customers).

Planning jointly should always mean coordination and leveraging where possible. But it must never mean compromises in execution.

The PR plan is now going to be the basis for all further PR measurements.

No PR plan - no objectives. No objectives - no measures. No measures - no control.

Writing a PR plan is a skill in itself and will not be covered in this book. Therefore in the following chapters only one important rule is followed: a PR plan that does not address the evaluation of PR is not worth the paper it is written on.

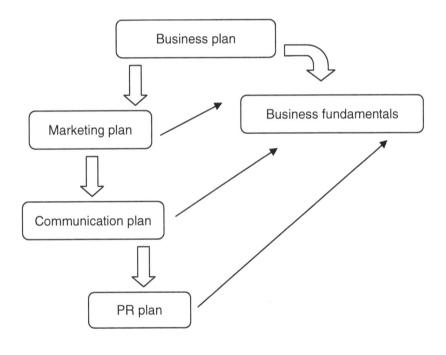

Figure 2.1 Planning structure

THE CONCEPT OF A BALANCED SCORECARD

In 1992, Kaplan and Norton published their works on operational measures that are the drivers of future financial performance. The basic idea was to define a measurement matrix that was going beyond just traditional financial measures. Financial criteria like revenue, profit or ROI were considered to be symptoms, not causes, of success or failure. Also, it became obvious that certain goals could not be described directly in terms of dollar values. An example would be the goal to reach a break-even time for products within a certain defined period – a goal that Hewlett-Packard pioneered and continues to follow successfully.

In fact, Kaplan and Norton developed a structure, in which monetary criteria were only one of four fields to influence PR effectiveness and PR efficiency. The four fields they defined are:

1. Employees

2. Processes

3. Customers

4. Financials.

All four areas are interdependent and for all four areas key questions can be asked to identify relevant criteria for a given situation:

EMPLOYEES

Kaplan and Norton base their ideas on the assumption that the capabilities, the enthusiasm or motivation, the loyalty and the inventiveness of the employees are key success factors – not only in PR. As a consequence, subjects like education and innovation need to be addressed. So, a question to answer in this field is 'How can we constantly improve our PR work?'

PROCESSES

This area covers aspects like communication processes within the company. It also addresses everything defined in a service level agreement with your company internal stakeholders, planning processes, timeliness, turnaround times for projects or inter-action with PR agencies. The question to answer in this area is 'What processes are relevant to guarantee success?'

CUSTOMERS

A typical question in this field is 'What behaviour change do we want to achieve in our target audience?' This question is obviously driven by goals such as creating brand awareness, preference or ultimately the intention to have our customers purchase our products.

A very loose interpretation of the term 'customer' would also allow it to be defined as the company internal stakeholders in our PR activities. This could be our marketing department or our CEO. A reason for taking this approach is often the statement that the PR department cannot be made accountable for the customers' behaviour – or at least its influence cannot be separated out. Assuming your customers are your internal stakeholders would mean that your goals could easily be different from assuming you measure yourself against the impact you have on the real customers. In fact, the goals would quickly be inbound focused and could end up becoming an internal justification of the PR department's existence.

Even though this approach is common practice in a range of companies, we would like to discourage you from following it for two reasons. The first one is that you can easily end up losing focus on your outbound charter, and the second one is that you would lose one of the major values of a PR department. In your function you should be the advocate for the outside world in your company. You should be able to take an 'outside looking in' view at your company and you should be able to provide a feedback mechanism from the external world into your organisation. All these aspects of your work could be overlooked if you focus too much on internal goals.

FINANCIALS

The simple question we need to ask ourselves in the PR department is 'How do those judge us who provide us with our PR budgets?' So, we should look into our own cost management. But, it should go without saying that a PR department cannot be made responsible for the company's overall financial situation and cannot be measured against it.

Kaplan and Norton's 'balanced scorecard' is a set of measures that addresses all four areas introduced above. 'Score' can be considered an abbreviation for strategic clarity, cascaded measures, objective setting, results driven and executing change, a term that describes the underlying principles of their approach very well.

Similar to the set of business fundamentals, the balanced scorecard is supposed to be a simple set of measures that provides a quick overview of the entire performance of an entity, in this case of the PR department. The number of line items, however, is bigger than in the business fundamentals. A good approach would be to look into four to five measures per area as defined above. So, in total we are looking at roughly 15 to 20 line items for a balanced scorecard of a PR department. You should understand that fewer is possible, but then the balanced approach may be compromised. Also, more is possible, but then you may lose focus on the breakthrough goals.

Each of the 15 to 20 goals must be derived from the company's overall directions. For each of them a measurable value needs to be defined that can be tracked over time. The current value and the target value that you are supposed to achieve in a given timeframe need to be known. And finally, you need to agree on actions that you will take to achieve your goals, and you need to be able to track your progress over time, for example, through quarterly or monthly performance reviews.

You will find a template for a balanced scorecard in Appendix D.

THE OUTPUT–OUTGROWTH–OUTCOME MODEL

Dr Walter Lindenmann developed a hierarchical model to measure the results of PR activities that is still widely adopted today. It is based on measuring results on three levels which he refers to as 'output', 'outgrowth' and 'outcome'.

Dr Lindenmann in his resource booklet for the Institute for Public Relations *Public Relations Research for Planning and Evaluation* described those terms in details:

> Outputs are usually the short-term, or immediate, results of a particular communications programme or activity. More often than not, outputs represent what is readily apparent to the eye. Outputs measure how well an organisation presents itself to others, the amount of attention or exposure that organisation receives. In media or press efforts, outputs can be the total numbers of stories, articles, or 'placements' that appear in the media … the total number of 'impressions' – that is, the number of those who might have been exposed to the story … as well as an assessment of the overall content of what has appeared. Media content analysis is one of the principal methodologies used to measure media outputs.

In very simple terms, the output level covers the basic results of PR work. This would include the number of journalists attending a press conference or the articles written by the journalists.

The second level, the outgrowth level, focuses more on the content and the question of whether the content was well understood by the target audience. The target audience in this context can either be the journalists themselves or their readers, the ultimate target audience, the customers.

Finally, the third level called 'outcome level' examines changed behaviour of the target audience. Again, this could apply to the journalists and their attitude towards your company, or their readers and for example their buying behaviour.

According to Dr Lindenmann: 'As important as it might be to measure communications outputs, it is far more important to measure communications outgrowths and outcomes. These measure whether target audience groups actually received the messages directed at them … paid attention to them … understood the messages … and retained the messages in any shape or form.' He continues: 'It is usually much more difficult and, generally, more expensive, to measure communicaons outgrowths and outcomes than it is to measure communications outputs. This is because more sopisticated data-gathering research tools and techniques are required.'

An example of a set of measurements across these three levels would be the following:

Output: Number of generated articles as taken from a clipping service.
Outgrowth: Feedback from a target audience per survey.
Outcome: Attitude change as taken from a comparison of two surveys (one before, one after the PR campaign).

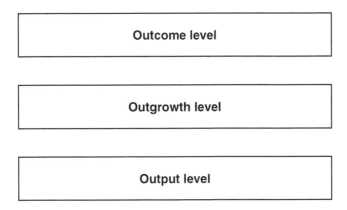

Figure 2.2 Lindenmann's measurement model

The 'Lindenmann-model' is an excellent model that summarises all aspects of measuring PR or even communication in general. For practical purposes, it may be easier sometimes, though, to look into certain aspects separately.

In particular, there are two aspects of measurement that we would like to address in an isolated way. The first one is on company internal measures and the second one is on measuring the relationship of your company with the journalists.

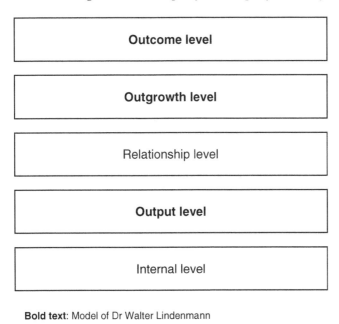

Bold text: Model of Dr Walter Lindenmann

Figure 2.3 Five measurement levels

Any PR activity can now be measured on all five levels. In the following chapters, we will look into five typical PR measurements:

- measuring the results of an interview
- measuring the results of a press conference
- measuring the results of a PR campaign
- measuring long-term results

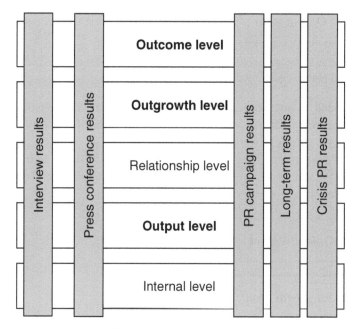

Bold text: Model of Dr Walter Lindenmann

Figure 2.4 Evaluation of 'vertical PR activities'

This approach can be considered as measuring a specific PR activity on a more tactical level. While Lindenmann addresses the segmentation of the evaluation process generically 'horizontally', we will look into the evaluation of 'vertical PR activities'.

We believe that this approach will be helpful in the day-to-day PR work in an organisation.

MEASUREMENT BUDGETS

Yes, it is unfortunate – to measure your PR performance does cost money! PR budgets are never sufficient. Or, in other words: the budget is always a limiting factor in PR.

So, you are in a dilemma now. Do you spend part of your tight budget on another PR project, or do you spend it on evaluating the results of your past projects?

We hope this book will convince you that you should indeed spend some money on evaluation. And, in fact, you should consider this to be an investment in the future. Often people hesitate to spend money on PR measurements. They would rather spend their budget on developing a PR plan for a new project. However, since the communication process is a circle, an investment into measurements equals an investment into a new PR project. Basically, we learn from the past in order to avoid the same mistakes in the future and to make our future activities more efficient and effective.

Now the question remains how we should split our budget between execution and evaluation. What split is reasonable? Experience shows that roughly a 90/10 approach is very reasonable. In other words: 10 per cent of your budget should be dedicated to evaluation. (In *PR Week*'s Proof Campaign, they also argue for a target spend on research and evaluation (R&E) equivalent to 10 per cent of the budget.) This would include a clipping service, a detailed feedback report, an event summary and regular media analysis reports.

In a cooperative work of *PRCA*, *IPR* and *PR Week* a more detailed specification of the size of the measurement budget was defined. They make it dependent on the overall size of the PR budget.

Total budget	Budget percentage for measurement	
	Minimum	Optimum
Up to $50k	10	12
$50–$100k	7	10
$100k–$500k	5	7
Above $500k	3	5

Table 2.1 Measurement budget
(Source: Research and evaluation toolkit, *PRCA, IPR, PR Week*)

It is interesting to note that the size of the measurement budgets in our industry has significantly increased over time. According to the 21 March, 2002 edition of *The Measurement Standard*, published by KD Paine & Partners, the spending on PR measurement has increased over the past 15 years from about 3 per cent to about 10 per cent.

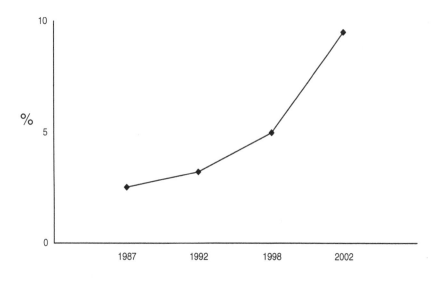

Figure 2.5 Average percentage budget spent on measurement
(Source: KD Paine and Partners)

This increase in spending on measurement is probably also due to an increasingly better understanding of the impact of the PR process being a circle (see Figure 1.1). Put simply: learning from experience will help to manage future projects more effectively and will save resources in general and budgets in particular. One of the most obvious aspects is the clear definition of your target audience at the beginning of a campaign. Doing your homework in this respect well upfront will allow you to define the media you want to address with your story and the proper media mix in a more targeted way. You will be able to avoid overlaps or gaps, both leading to an inefficient use of your resources.

MEASURING A PR AGENCY AS A VENDOR/CLIENT

It is a trend in our industry today that vendors focus on their core competencies. Outsourcing has become very popular. And even though an end to this trend has already been predicted, PR has typically always been dependent on external agency support – since it has never been considered a core competency of most corporations.

Selecting an agency is already a challenge – and measuring agencies on an ongoing basis is yet another one. But again, both tasks are very closely related to each other, since they are both based on the initial objectives that have been defined.

PR agencies have specialised on certain tasks. Some focus on consumer PR, some on PR for commercial customers. Some agencies focus on executive PR, some on promoting products or services. Many agencies focus exclusively on certain industries that may demand special skill sets. Some agencies have specialised on crisis PR and others only on evaluation.

Regardless of the requested service, the selection of an agency already defines the criteria that are used afterwards to measure the agency.

Attention should be paid to several general criteria from the start. They include for example the question of whether the cultures of the two companies match. They should not be on two opposite ends of a spectrum. On the other hand, an agency should not be just a carbon copy of your own company, since this could easily result in the agency not being able to inspire you, or to provide creative ideas that you could not have developed in-house.

The above is based on the assumption that you expect your agency to be creative, to consult with you, to inspire you, to challenge you. Yes, we agree with you that it would be much easier to have your agency simply execute your plans. But if this is what you expect from a PR agency you should ask yourself if this could not be done using less expensive resources. For example, a PR event may also be carried out with the help of an events agency or a logistics agency.

A PR agency can be selected – and measured – by several criteria. There are two very human ones, though, for which it is very difficult to find a formula.

The first one is probably one of the golden rules every client needs to take into account:

Every agency can only be as good as it is briefed.

The best agency cannot be successful if you do not brief them appropriately – and if you do not give them proper access to information and people.

The second aspect is as important to keep in mind.

An agency can only be as good as the individuals working in it.

As a result, you need to be very careful when choosing an agency. The agency will probably send a very experienced representative to do the sales pitch to you and they will impress you a lot. Be aware, though, that you will probably work with different individuals afterwards. Only if they are convincing as well, do you have an agency with whom you will want to work.

But then, again, be careful when you see changes to members of the team working for you. That's the time when you want to make sure you are able to measure the impact of that change.

But let us go back to the criteria you need to define when selecting your PR agency. You need to identify criteria that will enable you to rank the agencies that pitch for your contract. Be aware that you will come up with two sets of criteria, the professional ones and a second set that we would call 'others' lacking a better description.

You would then need to identify a points scheme and rank the agencies you evaluate against it. The criteria and points scheme (1 being unacceptable, 5 being excellent) may look like Table 2.2:

Professional criteria					
Market knowledge	1	2	3	4	5
Experience/credentials	1	2	3	4	5
International experience (Europe and worldwide)	1	2	3	4	5
Skills portfolio (for example, release writing, project handling)	1	2	3	4	5
Professional appearance	1	2	3	4	5
Communication skills	1	2	3	4	5
Innovative	1	2	3	4	5
Reliability	1	2	3	4	5
Flexibility (for example, manpower, plan changes)	1	2	3	4	5
Staff (for example, "seniority", in-house skills)	1	2	3	4	5
Understanding of our briefing material/our requirements	1	2	3	4	5
Openness (for example, ability to listen or admit knowledge gaps)	1	2	3	4	5
Proactiveness (consult vs. plain execution on demand)	1	2	3	4	5
Other criteria:					
Did the (designated) account manager present – as requested?	1 (No)				5 (Yes)
Compatibility with your own company's culture	1	2	3	4	5
Company's (financial) stability	1	2	3	4	5
Dedication/enthusiasm shown in presentation	1	2	3	4	5
Style of presentation	1	2	3	4	5
Handouts/written documentation	1	2	3	4	5
Individuals (subjective)	1	2	3	4	5
Connections (for example, to creatives or events agencies)	1	2	3	4	5
Potential conflict with other clients?	1 (Yes)	2	3	4	5 (No)

Table 2.2   PR agency evaluation criteria

You may also want to weigh up the criteria and have the top ones loaded with more points than others.

The future measurement of your PR agency should be based on two inputs. The first one is given by the criteria you initially defined as described above. The second one is the generic set of PR measurements as described in this book. This, however, needs to be looked at in more detail: you can only measure your agency against your PR success if you have empowered them appropriately to be able to accomplish their task.

CHAPTER 3

Measuring the Results of a Press Interview

A smart conversation is Eden.
Khalif Ali Ben Ali Thaleb (602-661)

A contact with a journalist can happen as the result of either of the following:

- You request a meeting with a journalist, that is, you invite a journalist for a meeting or interview, or

- The journalist asks for an interview.

It is obvious that the intentions of both parties are very different for each of these scenarios.

INTERVIEWS REQUESTED BY THE PR DEPARTMENT

At first glance, it seems to be easier to measure the results of an interview that was requested by yourself rather than by the journalist; you are able to define your goals beforehand in as much detail as you wish.

Here is a selection of reasons why you may request a meeting with a journalist:

- To introduce your new product or service.

- You may want to make an early unit available to the publication for testing.

- You want to promote one of your executives in the media.

- You want to inform and educate the journalist on current industry trends or new technologies.

- You want to address the business press with a business update of your company.

- You intend to inform your local community acknowledging that they contribute to your company's perception in the public.

- Others (sponsorships, employee's promotion, and so on).

We now look more closely at each of these reasons:

1a.   One of the most common reasons is probably the introduction of a new product, service or solution. You want to inform the trade press of the news, so that they can inform their readers. In this case you would expect an article in the 'new products' column. You would want the headline of the article to address your main message, for example, 'best price', 'best performance', 'ease-of-use', 'latest design', or similar.

Additional objectives may include:

- The journalist compares your product favourably with competitive products.

- You want your brand name to be mentioned as often as possible.

- Your target markets are referred to in the article.

- You want a picture of your product to accompany the article.

- You want to keep a continuous relationship either with an individual journalist or with a certain publication.

'Hidden agendas' could be one or more of the following:

- You want to position one of your spokespeople in the industry. In that case, you would want to have a reference to him in the article – ideally even a quote or a picture.

- You want a reference in the article to other products from your company.

- You want a reference in the article to a business partnership with another company.

1b.   For a product introduction, it should also be researched if certain publications do product reviews. You may want to make an early trial unit available to the publication for testing.

The intention is obviously to get a detailed review of your product into the paper. The advantage of such an article is that it typically covers your product in great detail and allows all the positive features to be highlighted. Unfortunately, it is also a great opportunity for the press to highlight all the negative aspects of your product. So, it is a double-edged sword.

For a product review, you only have a limited opportunity to influence the tone of the resulting article. An interview only rarely happens. It is more likely that your technical staff will make contact with the journalist for support purposes. It should be a golden rule that you will never hand out product to the media for review without having identified support engineers. These people need to be fully media trained and understand the message you want to get across.

Measures for product reviews include:

- Be aware of scheduled reviews in the media. Ideally, no significant product review should be published that does not cover your product – unless you consciously want to avoid them (see also Chapter 7 about crisis communication).

- Define beforehand, how your product should score against the competition and compare the result with your initial expectations. It should be noted here that the results of this comparison are good inputs for the marketing organisation and to a lesser extent for the PR department.

- Define the key features of your product that should be highlighted in the review and compare them with the actual article written.

2.   You want to promote one of your executives in the media.

The key question you should ask yourself before you start promoting a company executive is why do you want to do this?

There are several obvious reasons why you may want to promote an individual. In certain industries, the value and the brand of a company are closely connected to an individual. A popular fashion designer, for example, operates as the figurehead of his company. It would be impossible to avoid promoting him in the media. Often the demand from the press to get access to this person is higher than the amount of access that can be offered – in a similar way to pop stars and other celebrities.

In addition, in industries that are not necessarily known for employing eccentric creatives or artists, certain individuals have created a charisma around them that make them an icon and the media want to publish every single word they say. Microsoft's Bill Gates, Sun Microsystem's Scott McNealy, Virgin's Richard Branson or GE's (former) Jack Welch are but a few examples.

However, there are two main guidelines that should always be followed when promoting speakers to the media:

- When looking for a speaker, do not just look in the direction of your CEO or Managing Director. Often the true 'PR stars' are lower down in the hierarchy.

- It is a proven fact that the quality of a press article is enhanced significantly whenever a company spokesperson is quoted – as long as he is 'on message' or has been trained to be.

There are several instances when the promotion of an individual is not justified.

The most popular one is the sole intention of being famous. This goal is well justified for politicians[1] or artists. Companies, however, should not forget that they generate their revenue from selling their products, not from selling their employees – unless you are the PR manager of a football club and your goal is to 'sell' one of your players at a high price to another club.

On the other hand, however, there are also several very good reasons why you may want to promote one of your spokespeople in the media. The one of most benefit to your company is to position one of your employees – it does not always need to be the CEO or a top executive – as an *industry speaker*.

The difference between a 'company spokesperson' and an 'industry speaker' is of prime importance here!

The job of a company spokesperson is to position their own company in the right way. His goal must always be to create headlines for that company.

An industry speaker is a respected and trusted person within that industry who understands the business and the trends. He is usually contacted whenever a second opinion is needed. Journalists choose to refer to him whenever they want to validate their own research or to comment on a statement from a competitor. And they want that statement presented in an honest way. Unqualified bashing of the competition spoils your speaker's reputation. Note that it never hurts your company when you say something nice about your competition at the right time. There are other ways to promote your own company than talking negatively about others. (An exception could be a market with only two competitors.)

A clear measure of a good spokesperson is the number of interview requests they get from the media. Once you have initially introduced your expert, that is, once you have sown the seeds, in an ideal world, you should become purely reactive. The demand for a bad spokesperson, in return, is only very small.

3.   You want to inform and educate the journalist on current industry trends or new technologies.

Just as you need to invest in your children's education or on training for company employees, education of the media is also an important area of investment.

The intention here is not to generate immediate coverage. It could still happen, but it would be the exception. 'Educational sessions' should not always be considered to be formal meetings following a defined agenda. In fact, this

---

1   Today, the media are a dominating factor for the success or failure of political campaigns. This became very obvious in several elections for the US presidency and also most recently in the election of the governor of the US state of California. So, elections are not just generic examples anymore for measurable success (see, for example, Albert Oeckl: *Handbuch der Public Relations*, Süddeutscher Verlag München), but can also be considered as a modern form of PR evaluation.

would also be the exception. It is much more likely that you, for example, invite journalists to an informal monthly get-together over a beer or a glass of wine – whatever is culturally correct. You may also want to invite selected journalists to attend customer product trainings – if that particular journalist is interested and if he or she has a sufficient level of basic knowledge.

The goal in these sessions is to make journalists understand that you are a player in a certain market. Also, it allows you to position your own company as an industry thought leader, a company that understands trends and customer needs. Moreover, you have the opportunity to position your speakers as visionaries or industry spokespeople.

The desired outcome of these activities should be for example to be referenced or even highlighted in feature articles that could appear at any time between now and up to six or nine months from now. You would have clearly failed to achieve that outcome, if an article was written by one of the attending journalists addressing topics your company is involved in, but your company is not even mentioned in the article.

4.   You want to address the business press with a business update of your company.

The news hook could be the regular announcement of your financial results, a restructuring of your company, an acquisition, a strategic partnership with another vendor, a new go-to-market strategy, a major customer win, your company's investment plan for your region or a significant increase of the company's market share. In some cases, a new image campaign and/or a new significant advertising or promotional campaign could also be the trigger for an interview with the business media.

You can measure resulting articles by many criteria. They include:

- *Tone*
  Note that the tone can be perceived very subjectively. It is always best to have this evaluated by an external person judging the article from the point of view of a reader, and not the company (the vendor) itself.

- *Headline*
  The headline should be to the point. Ideally, your main message is covered in the headline.

- *Placement in the publication*
  An article on the front page is worth significantly more than the same sized article buried somewhere on a left hand page in the middle of the publication.

- *Article size*
  It is probably needless to say that the size of an article contributes significantly to its impact on the reader. This is true for any topic. For example,
  an article covering a straightforward product introduction can range from
  a brief standard mention like 'company xyz now offers a new product that
  is 10 per cent less expensive and 20 per cent faster' all the way to a long
  article profiling your company and for example embedding your new
  product into your company's strategic product roadmap.

- *Judgement of your company*
  Any long-term prediction of your company's development should be
  watched out for very carefully. A negative comment in the business press
  can be very damaging, since it will impact on the attitude of investors,
  influencers and decision makers.

- *Positive quote from analyst*
  The value of an article increases significantly with the quote of an independent analyst. In the business press, this would typically be a financial
  analyst – but depending on the topic, industry analysts are referenced as well.

- *Quotes are exactly as intended*
  Compare the quotes from the article with what you intended to convey
  according to your initial plan. If your spokesperson was quoted with a
  statement that you would consider only a side note, then you did not get
  your main message across properly.

- *Message and content are appropriate for target audience*
  Check if your message was packaged correctly to appeal to the reader base
  of the publication. For example, if the article only refers to your company
  as a supplier for the financial services industry, but the publication is read
  primarily by executives in the telecom or service provider space, you have
  delivered inappropriate content to the journalist.

We will discuss these criteria in more detail later in this book.

5.   You intend to inform your local community, acknowledging that they contribute
     to your company's perception in the public eye.

     Many larger corporations focus their PR activities on national or international
     campaigns. They try to promote their products across borders into the markets
     that have been identified.

     At the same time, they need to take into account that they probably play an
     important role in their local environment, their local community. This local
     engagement could range from being a sponsor of the local volleyball team to
     being a key factor in the local employment figures.

The company could also be a strong driving factor in the local economy overall. Maybe it makes suppliers move to the area and therefore not only generate jobs itself, but also create new jobs indirectly.

Your company may open a new office building or a new manufacturing site – both should be of interest to the local press. Charity or sponsorships of educational institutions (schools, universities) can also provide a hook to get local – or even national and international press – interested in featuring your company.

All the above shows that you should not underestimate the power your company may have in the local economy.

Measuring your PR success in the local media is very different from your other measurement schemes promoting your products. You may experience much more openness towards your company than you experience elsewhere. You may see a certain pride shown through having a company of national or even international visibility located in their neighbourhood.

Your PR measures should therefore be different. You should not compare your coverage in the local media with the coverage of your main competitor, but with the coverage other local companies enjoy. You want to ensure that you are indeed integrated into the local community.

Besides the local aspect there is also a more personal angle involved. You should expect to have a much closer personal relationship with the reporter of the local newspaper than you would have with the editor of an international magazine whom you potentially meet only once a year.

6.   Other reasons.

It is worthwhile acknowledging that there are many other reasons for your company to proactively address the media.

You may, for example, sponsor a local sports team or an individual sportsman.

There is another reason that is often overlooked: the promotion of your employees' competence in their respective functions. For example, your HR manager may be able to contribute to public discussions related to the unemployment rate, workers' skills demanded in the industry, or compensation packages.

Your R&D director may want to comment on scientific research in the respective academic publications. Or your manufacturing manager wants to address new processes on the factory floor in the respective media.

All these PR activities and the resulting interviews with the press are not intended to promote your company or a product of your company directly. However, they provide background support as you build an image for your company and communicate your company's competence in many directions.

Measures for these kinds of interviews should be different from the ones previously discussed and may include the following:

- You should check to see if the core values of your company have been communicated. These could for example be high quality standards, the value of the employees, the inventiveness of the company, the company's culture, or new working models.

- The competence of your company's employees should come across in the generated articles.

- Indirectly (!) leave a positive image of the company.

INTERVIEWS REQUESTED BY THE PRESS

Let us now turn to those interviews that are requested by the media.

We will assume for now that the press has not requested an interview with a representative from your company because of a crisis situation. (This scenario will be discussed later.)

So, you should congratulate yourself on being in the situation of receiving requests from the press for interviews. It shows that the PR work you have done in the past has paid off. It shows that either your company is recognised as a leading player in the market - or it shows that one of your spokespeople has elevated himself to the level of respected industry speaker whose opinion is considered to be relevant.

Despite the fact that being contacted by a journalist is a positive sign (and the number of such enquiries itself could indeed be a good measure of the interest you stimulated in the media), it also includes a high risk. The challenge is not to be in control. Initially you do not know the reason for the call - and therefore the measure for the interview and the outcome can only be very generic.

Your first goal needs to be to identify the reason for the call. In other words, your prime measure should be to not get surprised during the interview itself. It is not necessary to know every single question in advance (even though some companies follow that strategy – much to the despair of the media), however the initial reason for the interview request, the topic and the initial opinion of the journalist should be assessed before the interview.

For example: we mentioned earlier that companies listed on the stock exchange publicly report their business results on a quarterly basis. These companies normally have 'quiet periods' or 'blackout periods', during which time they cannot make any statement about their financial situation. This period usually lasts for one month before the announcement. This circumstance needs to be considered when you are preparing to answer press interview requests. In other words, you need to make sure that you have evaluated all the aspects of the true reasons for a journalists' call.

For the interview itself, one main objective is valid:

No surprises!

A very basic measure is being able to meet the deadline of the journalist. For the traditional paper press the deadline is driven by the editorial deadline and closing date. For online publications deadlines tend to be much tighter. Articles can be published by the journalist at almost any point in time. So, his deadline is much more driven by his goal to beat the competition and have an article out before them. Therefore, an online journalist may request information within minutes rather than hours.

You may consider measuring several additional aspects. In doing so, you need to separate the evaluation of the interview itself from the evaluation of the output of the interview.

During the interview there are criteria to which you need to pay attention: like your spokesperson's ability to respond to questions and to get his main message across in his answers; the length of the interview; questions asked by the journalist; and the ability of your spokesperson to stay in or to gain control. Finally, changing attitudes of the journalist are a strong indicator of your performance on the outgrowth level.

Evaluation of the output has been discussed before. It would be interesting to compare the output with the impression you were left with after the interview itself. Especially in the instance where the journalist was very open and friendly at the interview, but then wrote an extremely negative article. This would make it very clear that there is room for improving your relationship with that journalist!

CHAPTER 4

Measuring the Results
of a Press Conference

News is something that someone, somewhere wants to suppress;
all the rest is advertising.
Lord Northcliffe, founder of the Daily Mail *(1865-1922)*

A few years ago, we were involved in press activities at the world's largest IT trade show CeBIT (Center for Office and Information Technology) in Hanover, Germany. Those of you who have ever attended the event know that it is a zoo that can only be kept under control following strict guidelines. Therefore, when it was discovered that our press conference was to take place in parallel with one of our main competitors, we were concerned, but it was too late for changes. We found ourselves in the situation of having to compete for our target audience. So, apart from all the communication goals we had in mind, suddenly we were faced with a more elementary challenge: attract an audience to listen to us. In other words: get bums on seats – and, if compromises have to be made: get the right bums on seats.

The basic measure was clear. We selected a strategy and executed it. We approached the situation from two angles. First of all, we decided to use the situation as an opportunity and brought messages from various parts of the company together in order to appear as one '800 pound gorilla' instead of many little monkeys. Secondly, we chose a unique invitation process in the style of a teaser campaign, sending out keys to the journalists – keys which they were asked to bring to the press conference in order to open a door to a little treasure. Well, how curious would you be to discover what is behind the locked door that you already have the key to?

The result was that we hosted about three times more journalists than we had initially anticipated. Tables and chairs had to be removed from the room in order to make space for the standing participants. The journalists enjoyed the content, wrote excellent articles about it – and they all brought their key to pick up their little treasure, a survival kit for the CeBIT Fair. Needless to say, our competitor had a very disappointing press conference that day!

This one example shows that what we have learned in the previous chapters is a prerequisite for this one, but this chapter will go one step beyond what we have discussed earlier. Press interviews can be considered to be a part of a press conference and, at the same time, measuring the results of a press conference is akin to measuring the results of a special PR campaign or a part thereof. The main difference would be that a press conference is an event at a defined point in time whereas a PR campaign can last for a longer period. However, even though a press conference is a singular event, it should not be viewed as such in the context of the overall communication process. A press conference needs to be integrated into the overall communication strategy of the company. It needs to be consistent with earlier PR activities and it needs to be in line with other communication activities of the company.

For example, your messages need to be consistent over time and across the company. Also, you need to choose from your various communication tools (press release, interview, press conference) consistently depending on your specific announcement. For example, you do not necessarily want to announce a minor product enhancement in a worldwide press conference, and then only let the world know about your company's new CEO in a press release. In other words, you must select your communication tactics depending on the news value of your announcement.

Before we go into the details of measurement criteria, we need to acknowledge that there are two fundamentally different types of press conference that cannot be treated with the same measures.

The first type is probably the most common one. This is a press conference in an environment where you do not have complete control, for example a press conference held at a major trade show. The above example of the CeBIT Fair obviously falls into this category. Here you will be competing with other press conferences held by many vendors. The attending journalists have not come to the event specifically to see your company's presentation and are completely free to decide what event they want to go to and what to skip. Journalists will not register in advance to attend your event, so you can only count on their participation at the event itself.

The second type provides your company with exclusive access to invited journalists. You may have brought them to a special location, that is, you have a captive audience. The entire event follows your predefined agenda. In such an environment you obviously have much more access to the individual journalists. You can spend dedicated time on presentations, special interest group breakouts, interviews or product demonstrations. There are few escape routes for your journalists.

As discussed before, we can measure the results of a press conference on several levels. A good tool for achieving additional data from the participating journalists is a press questionnaire (see Appendix A for an example).

INTERNAL LEVEL

A standard first internal goal is to see that your participating executives are happy. However, before you join in their enjoyment, you should double check the cause of their excitement. It could easily be that their general happiness is caused by some very individual subjective incidents at the event. Maybe they are just delighted about the number of journalists that attended the event – but a closer look may show you that you missed the intended target audience. Or, an executive was particularly happy about a particular interview, which was not representative of the entire event.

Internally you may also want to check if all the logistics went smoothly. Did the AV equipment work properly? Did transportation work as planned? Was the press kit ready in time and handed out to everybody? Was the timing of the event okay? The number of logistical aspects to look after is endless. It is important to remember not to get lost in measuring them. Even though they are important, you did not invite the journalists simply to enjoy a glass of champagne served in style...

One internal criterion that should be of great interest to you, though, is the number of interviews facilitated at the press conference. Often vendors make the mistake of believing that a press conference is a one-hour presentation – full stop. Far from it! The presentation may only be the appetiser – and in fact it should be done in less than an hour. The main course for the journalists is delivered to the individual in a one-to-one interview or in a question-and-answer session. So, the number of interviews that were executed on the back of the initial presentation is typically a good measure of the true interest of the journalists. The more interviews that were conducted, the more you can be reassured that your message was got across and well understood. Still, the pure number of interviews conducted is a very mechanical measure that can only give an initial indication immediately after a press conference. A more detailed evaluation is definitely required later on.

TACTICAL OR OUTPUT LEVEL

Probably the most basic tactical measure for a press conference is the number of attending journalists. (By the way, your immediate check should be to compare the number of journalists attending with the number invited – see also below.) If it was just mass awareness of your announcement that was key, then this criterion might be an easy one to measure. Nevertheless, it does not necessarily translate into good bottom line results. It is more or less just a 'bums-on-seats' approach that can be achieved by flying journalists to a beautiful venue – a place they cannot really say no to – and wining and dining them. This approach should not really considered to be PR, even though the selection of an appropriate location is important for such an announcement, it should only support the announcement and not become bribery.

A good venue cannot be an excuse for poor content.

It is much more important to have the right target audience at your event. Therefore, a more realistic approach is to identify the journalists and publications beforehand and compare afterwards who from your initial wish list actually attended. When you do this comparison, don't just compare the names of the publications, but also the level of seniority of the participating journalists. You may discover that all your target publications attended, but only junior journalists were sent. You should accept this as proof that they did not expect significant news at your event.

RELATIONSHIP LEVEL

Despite the fact that you may often hear that relationships cannot be measured, there are many ways of measuring your relationship with journalists.

The first opportunity to have some feedback is right before the event itself by having a careful look into the journalists' reaction to your invitation. Do they respond immediately? Do they confirm their attendance right away? If so, it means that they trust you. They are convinced that they will not be wasting their time attending your event. They have probably had a good experience with your company before and know that you only request their attendance at an event when you really have something important to share with them. You should always bear in mind that attending a press conference is a significant investment on the journalist's behalf. They would only dedicate that much time to your event when they are sure that there will be a good return on that investment.

Apart from noting the number of acceptances it would also be interesting to see what the reasons are for not attending. Do they even come back to you at all? And if so, is the negative response to your invitation a valid one or just a polite excuse, leaving the impression that they consider other activities to be more important than your event? If they simply cannot attend your event – maybe just for logistical or personal reasons or because that time slot is already booked – a journalist would still be interested in receiving the information in a timely fashion and/or following it up at another time with a briefing (like a phone-based interview) by one of your company's spokespeople.

It should also be noted that the number of acceptances can indicate if the topic of the press event was explained and positioned correctly in the invitation, or if the information in the invitation letter was not stimulating any interest at all to attend.

At the event itself, it is always important to collect feedback from the journalists. This can happen either informally through small talk during a break or over lunch or dinner, or in a very formal way, for example, with the help of a feedback form (see Appendix A).

If you prefer the informal way, you must ensure that you have a sufficient number of journalists from whom you can draw a conclusion. Also, you must listen and document the feedback very carefully. And, you must ensure that the feedback is collected in a consistent way, that is, you should ask the same questions to the various journalists you talk to. Ideally, you would collect feedback not just on your own, but also with the help of some of your colleagues. That way, there is a better chance of avoiding the trap of hearing only what you want to hear. And, the journalists may be more or less open with different people.

Another measure could be the level of engagement you see from the journalists at the event. Do they interact with your spokespeople or do they look for discussions? This would be a very good sign that they are interested in the topic and the particular announcement. Or do they stay passive? In which case they probably did not connect with your message. Either you did not adapt your message to their respective fields of interest or your announcement was simply not as important as you initially thought. It could also be that you simply set your expectations too high.

CULTURAL ASPECTS

At this point it is important to note that there are cultural differences that you need to pay attention to. Delivering the same message with the same speakers to journalists with the same fields of interest could cause very different reactions in different countries. The obvious challenge would be language barriers. Assume you deliver your message in English somewhere in Europe. In the UK, you would have no issues whatsoever, in Scandinavia you should feel comfortable as well. But the more you go south or east in Europe, the more you need to be prepared for your audience to prefer the content to be delivered in their local language.

But even if we disregard the language challenge, there are still cultural differences that cause your audience to react differently to the same presentations. For example, Finnish or Dutch audiences are typically more conservative and may not show a very strong reaction either way to your announcement. At the other end of the spectrum, you may find the British media – despite the fact that the British in general are considered to be more conservative than other nationalities.

If your announcement is related to technology, you will also discover that there are country-dependent differences in Europe. Journalists writing for the same type of publications from different countries will perceive the same presentation differently. Generally, the British press is interested more in business aspects, while the French or Russian press is more interested in technology details. (We have attended international press conferences where English journalists leave the room and complain afterwards that the content was far too 'techy'. At the same time, their French colleagues who write for publications with a similar focus and a similar target audience in their country would have liked to have seen even more technical details of the products. Apparently, when that happens your press conference was the right compromise for an international audience).

Another aspect that is subject to cultural differences is whether you are given access to an article for proofreading prior to publication. In several countries you would probably not even ask a journalist for that favour, in some other countries journalists would be comparatively open to the idea.

ATTITUDE AND PERCEPTION

The attitude and perception of a journalist can be positioned in a grid as in Figure 4.1.

Completing Figure 4.1 is still subjective to some degree, but it helps significantly to follow individual journalists around this grid over time. Your objective should always be to move a journalist, who you consider to be important for your business, to the upper right-hand corner of the diagram.

	Consistent and frequent			
Proactive outreach	Somewhat regular			
	Sporadic			
		Negative	Receptive	Publicly positive
		Attitude towards – or perception of – your company		

Figure 4.1 Attitude/perception grid

Depending on the current status, that is, the current position on the diagram, and the identified reasons for being there several trajectories are possible for developing the relationship with a journalist. A very typical trajectory should be initially to intensify the communication with a journalist, that is, move him up in the diagram.[1] This will not change his attitude immediately, that is, you should not expect him to move horizontally right away. What you should see – if you have done your job well – is a move towards the right that follows with a more or less significant latency. This effect is well known in physics and is called hysteresis. It applies to many biological or physical systems that operate with a built-in memory – including humans (see Figure 4.2).

In the same way, journalists should remain positive for a while even though you may need to reduce the number of contacts with them. Dissatisfaction should only become apparent later.

Alarm bells should ring, when a journalist suddenly starts to move left. In that case you or some of your messages have probably upset him. In a good relationship this should not catch you by surprise, but you should be aware of it right away and be able to react right away.

---

1 Never forget: The time journalists spend with you they are not spending with your competition.

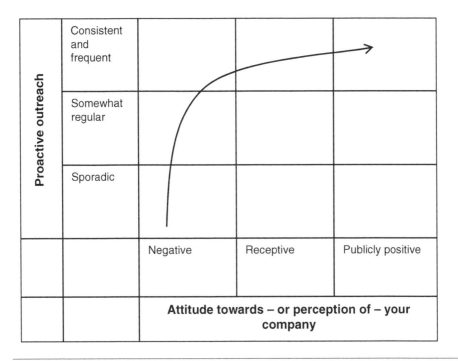

Figure 4.2   Attitude/perception grid – relationship development

TRUST

Another approach to measuring the level of your or your company's relationship with a journalist or a publishing house would be to introduce an index for *trust*. We should be aware of the fact that this is an abstract value that you need to animate depending on what you consider to be important to achieve your overall goals. We need to warn you, however, not to misinterpret the term trust! Do not mix it up with expectations towards journalists that would require them to compromise their independence!

Trust, as we understand it, includes a journalist's qualities like:

- openness towards messages from your company

- being unprejudiced

- fair coverage

- not being opinionated

- consult second opinions where appropriate

- shares values with yourself and/or your company

- ideally, admits the importance of the company's business and its presence in the market.

You should expect to be able to influence a journalist's trust in many ways. An obvious one is to stay in close contact with him or her. However, a diagram like Figure 4.3 will show you that the frequency with which you meet the journalist is not the only influencing parameter. If it was, all journalists should appear in a narrow band along the diagonal in the diagram.

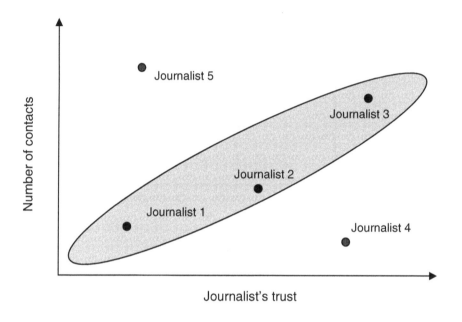

Figure 4.3 A journalist's trust

In Figure 4.3, the journalists 1 to 3 seem to follow the pattern where their relationship towards you is directly dependent on the number of contacts you make with them. Staying in contact makes you a good source for the journalist: you are easy to access and a source who provides good information for their readers.

According to the figure, journalist 4 puts a lot of trust in you even though the number of contacts is low. You can speculate why this is the case. Maybe the number of contacts is low because the content you provide is not in the focus of the publication they write for, but is still interesting to them. Maybe they put trust in all vendors. Maybe you compensated the number of contacts with the quality of contacts you made with them. For example, you may have given them exclusive access to a high-level executive at some point in time. But, whatever it was, you should try to identify the cause of their behaviour and transfer it to your relationship with other journalists, if possible.

Journalist 5 is on the other side of the spectrum. You seem to spend a lot of time working with them and developing a good relationship, but it does not seem to pay dividends. Maybe they write opinionated articles against your company or products, maybe they write about topics without even considering your company (even though you are a major player in that field). Maybe they disregard you because it is an editorial policy not to cover product introductions – but unfortunately that is the only thing you offer them. Again, many reasons could have caused that behaviour. Maybe your competitors' PR organisation has been very good in influencing this particular journalist. Or you need to look for an answer within your own organisation and you need to ask yourself questions like 'Do I provide the right services and/or messages to the journalist?' or 'Did I annoy them at some point in time?'

From Figure 4.3, journalist 5 is the one you focus your attention on, since they are probably the one who can be most damaging to your company.

To learn more about the aspect of trust, see also Chapter 6.

COVERAGE LEVEL

When it comes to measuring the coverage, all the standard criteria like number of articles or tone of the individual articles come into play again. The number of criteria by which you can split the coverage is almost endless. We will discuss some of the more important ones in the next chapter in the context of measuring results of a generic PR campaign.

There are only a few aspects you may want to look at specifically after a press conference. For example, you should evaluate to what degree the text of the articles actually referred to the press conference itself. Was the location mentioned? Was a specific spokesperson quoted? Were certain exhibits you had on display at the event referred to?

And, last but not least, was the article accompanied by picture material that either you provided generically or the journalist took themself?

If you do not see any reference to the event, you may want to ask yourself if the same coverage could not have been achieved in a different, maybe less expensive way. Could the distribution of a press release have had the same results? Why did you provide a photo opportunity that was not used?

OUTCOME LEVEL

Let us not forget that the ultimate goal is to influence the readers of the articles you generate through your PR activities. Therefore, the ultimate goal would also be to measure the attitude change of the readers.

The ideal situation would obviously be to make a direct connection from your press conference to the sales figures of your company. This is a very ambitious goal that is extremely difficult if not impossible to track for an individual press conference. Since your potential customers are influenced by many factors – articles generated by your press conference being only one of them – we want to address this topic in more detail in the next chapters. There, we will take a closer look at long-term trends that, for example, allow awareness and preference trends to be measured.

Nevertheless, there are certain scenarios that do allow you to draw conclusions about the impact of a press conference on your customers.

One scenario could be the following: you have introduced a product without accompanying the launch with a press conference and you have launched another product supported by a press conference. Assuming both products are comparable (addressing same markets, same audiences, same competitive situation, and so on), the different successes of the products may be tracked back to the different awareness you have generated with and without a press conference. However, this approach is not only very academic, but in doing so, you must also be able to exclude any other factor that could have caused the different market acceptance – a difficult task to accomplish. Especially, since:

Success always has many parents while failure is an orphan.

CHAPTER 5

Measuring the Results of a PR Campaign

Nothing is real unless it happens on television.
Daniel J. Boorstin (born 1914)

There are several classical definitions of what can be considered a PR campaign. We all know different PR tools that can be used to achieve certain business objectives over a defined time. Among them are interviews, teaser campaigns with press release pre-announcements, press briefings, press conferences of different sizes. The options are endless. For example, you may also consider announcing press awards on an annual basis, perhaps, on the day of your company's annual announcement of the financial results.

In a PR campaign we can combine the best suitable tools to reinforce a message and to gain a larger mind share of our target audience.

We would like to start this chapter with an example of a PR campaign which will help us introduce new measurement instruments closer to our everyday life.

We all have a special day in our life – our birthday. Just like human beings, our companies have a birthday – the day when the company is formally opened. We have the option to celebrate this only with the family, that is, internally with the employees. Or we use the opportunity wisely to celebrate a memorable day with our business partners, customers and the media. The PR department has a unique opportunity on this special day to communicate to the media the company business or its impact on the industry or the community. The list of topics is endless.

But, where do you start?

We had the chance to work on an interesting PR project involving the opening of the first official representative office of a major American IT corporation in Russia and the CIS – markets that are currently rapidly growing in this industry. The main question was how PR could help to inform the local market of the company plans to expand its business into Russia.

It is obvious that you can only open the office once. This opportunity will never return. Therefore, it was decided to develop a well thought through campaign. Since the company products were already known in the market and the main competitor already had an office in the region, it became even more important to make intense use of PR.

The target audience was well defined: the technical community – IT specialists in small and medium sized businesses as well as in larger corporations, and decision

makers of business customers as well as consumers, who buy PCs for the home. Therefore, it was essential to communicate to the 'techy' press *and* to business publications.

We decided to run a press conference to announce our company was starting
business in Russia and to introduce the new management team running the new office.
The fact was consciously pre-announced in a well-designed invitation campaign
including elegant invitation cards, phone invitations and e-mail reminders. A focus
was put on the fact that this was not just another product introduction, but included
presentations of business plans in order to also attract business journalists – a
significant challenge. A gala dinner followed the press conference with additional
entertainment, all creating an image for the company.

Another challenge was the fact that quite a lot of topics had to be presented to the
media. So, it became obvious that the press conference could only be part of a much
larger PR campaign. This included the involvement of celebrities, in this case the
president of the American Chamber of Commerce. Another part of the campaign was
the distribution of press material containing, for example, market information from
respected industry analysts and special pre-announcement interviews with key
business press journalists. These interviews took place earlier so that publications
with long lead times were able to publish at the most suitable time and coverage was
instantly available after the embargo date. Also, the immediate publication of online
articles resulted in a multiplier effect, that is, additional offline articles.

Another element of the PR campaign was the arrangement of numerous one-on-
one interviews with local office employees in order to create a long-lasting effect in the
media. Additional interviews with international executives were integrated under the
same 'umbrella' message.

Promotional campaigns with corporate advertising were executed in parallel to
make the impact of the campaign even stronger. A good and complete mix of communication tools were integrated into the campaign.

The campaign was a success. Even publications that initially were not convinced
sent their senior journalists. They were expected to pick up the press material and
leave after 15 minutes. In fact, they stayed throughout the entire event and became
heavily engaged in the topics under discussion.

And finally, the coverage of the campaign turned out to be about twice as high
compared to if we had only done a stand-alone press conference without any
supporting activities. And the quality was amazing – stories over several pages,
continuous coverage over a long period, strong headlines and the message was spot-on.

In this chapter we want to focus on measuring the output level as described in the
previous section. Even though it is not the primary goal in this section to look into the
outgrowth or even the outcome levels, we should still be aware of the fact that we need to
measure against initially defined goals – and these goals must take into account specifics
of the target audience. In particular, we must ensure that we use the proper media
channels to reach our identified target audience. Target audiences could be technical staff
or decision makers on the customer side. It could also be distribution channel partners,

investors or influencers and observers. Target audiences could also be segmented by customer type, that is, consumers, enterprises or small/medium sized businesses.

It is interesting to note that selection of the proper media channels is very much country dependent. International corporations, in particular, should be aware of the fact that a PR activity that for example worked in the US may not show the same results in France, or vice versa. Consumers not only react differently to the messages, but also are influenced by different media. For example, German customers tend to pay most attention to product reviews in the paper press, while Spanish customers tend to be most influenced by TV. In Russia there is a different phenomenon: there is a basic belief that a good product does not require promotions, therefore any obvious promotion campaigns may only cause suspicion and concern that the consumer has to pay for the company's advertising efforts, that is, the product is perceived to be too expensive.

Finally, it should be noted that the more you know about the demographics of your target audience, the better you can select the right media. In return, a good analysis of the press coverage generated afterwards can give you a very detailed picture of your results, dependent on the demographics of the target audience per publication.

We have already learned that output can be measured by volume and by quality.[1]

We will first look into the quantity aspect.

QUANTITY

As we have seen before, we can simply look into the *number of articles* generated by a PR campaign. We have also seen that this may not be a good measure since it does not tell us anything about the reach (or often referred to as 'mileage') of our campaign.

A typical approach is therefore to introduce a value called the *impression*. This factor is often also referred to as OTS ('opportunities to see'). The impression takes into account the circulation of the publication in which the article was published. On a first approach, the total number of impressions generated by a PR campaign is the sum of all articles multiplied by the respective circulation of the magazine they were published in:

$$I = \sum a^n b^n,$$

where

a is the number of articles in magazine n and
b is the circulation of magazine n.

---

1 We assume in this context that prominence is covered by quality features. Nevertheless, there is one more aspect to which you need to pay attention when you write your PR campaign feedback report. Do not only pay attention to what was achieved, but also to missed opportunities. You may have overlooked the fact that you could have integrated an industry event into your campaign, or your campaign would have been significantly more effective if you had supported it by activities not directly related to press campaigns, like, for example, customer direct mailings, advertising, or any other communication element. You will notice that you will greatly benefit from your observations when you start your next PR campaign.

This formula is probably self-explanatory and looks very easy to calculate. This is true for standard paper publications. An easy example would be a campaign that addressed four publications with circulations of 60 000 (publication A), 25 000 (publication B), 10 000 (publication C) and 4000 (publication D), respectively. Let us assume that one article was published in A, four articles in B, two in C and three in D. The number of impressions for this campaign would then be

$$I = 1 \cdot 60\ 000 + 4 \cdot 25\ 000 + 2 \cdot 10\ 000 + 3 \cdot 4000 = 192\ 000.$$

This can become more problematic for the broadcast media, since the audience reach varies according to programme day and time and the quota of the respective programme needs to be evaluated first (or for simplicity reasons, often an average is taken). It becomes a guessing game for online publications, however, where often the number of readers is not tracked, but only an estimate is available. Still, there are some measurements of audiences reach available for broadcasting and online media.

For example, we can use the same techniques as in advertising. We know that TV has the highest reach of all media, but it is still not necessarily 100 per cent of your target audience. So, often we end up with a random guess. In which case, research and statistical organisations that provide you with statistics of audience reach, as well as different indices such as GRP (gross rating points) are of great help.

With online publications you can always request statistics from their commercial department about web-publication audience reach, often measured by number of hits. The 'number of hits' is the total number of visitors to the web page, where, for example, an article is located. A second value often referred to is 'the number of hosts'. This figure describes the number of unique (!) visitors to the web page, as identified by the IP address of the computer from where they connected to the web page. Also, there are more sophisticated measures you may want to consider, such as CTR – click through rates and so on (It should be noted, though, that none of these figures are audited, that is, they can be very unreliable.)

There is a further difference between PR with online publications and working with the paper press. In particular, you need to be aware of the fact that information they publish is often reprinted on other sites and in off line magazines. Thus, there can easily be a multiplier effect on an article in one online publication. Also, online articles can provide you with customer or reader feedback much more easily since online articles are very often interactive.

Taking a more in-depth view you should acknowledge that every copy of a publication is exposed to more than just a single reader. An average value is defined for every publication. For standard publications, the value is between two and three. The enhanced formula for the impression value is therefore:

$$I = \sum x_n a_n b_n,$$

where

x is the average number of readers per copy of magazine n,
a is the number of articles in magazine n and
b is the circulation of magazine n.

Let us return to the above example with publications A, B, C and D and let us assume that publication A is read by only one reader per copy. Publication B, however, is read by three readers per copy. Finally, both C and D are read by two readers per copy. The number of impressions would then be:

$$I = 1 \cdot 1 \cdot 60\ 000 + 4 \cdot 3 \cdot 25\ 000 + 2 \cdot 2 \cdot 10\ 000 + 3 \cdot 2 \cdot 4000 = 424\ 000.$$

A comparison of both examples shows you that you may need to reevaluate your opinion of the value of the publications to your campaign when you look more closely into the number of readers per copy of the publication. In our example, the simple approach would have made you want to target publication A primarily. The enhanced calculation of the impression value, however, shows you that publication B will have a higher impact for your campaign.

It is sometimes extremely worthwhile taking a closer look into the impression value, especially when compared to the competitors' results, since it may reveal something about your competitors' PR strategy. For example, you may dominate the competition by number of articles generated at a particular time, yet they still have a larger number of impressions. This would tell you that they are targeting key publications with high circulations. Going one step further, this could mean that they achieve better results with less resources. Then, if you investigate further into the titles your competitors aim at, you may make some surprising discoveries.

For example, let us assume for a minute, that you are responsible for PR for commercial products. You have decided to address all those trade publications typically read by the users of your products. At the same time your competitor addresses the business press, which is not read by the users of your products, but the chief executive officer-level executives who make the purchase decisions for your products. Not only may the business publications have higher circulations than your 'special interest group publications', but they also address the target audience that has a direct impact on your sales figures. It should be noted that in reality borderlines are not as rigid as described above, since in many cases a proper mix of publications needs to be addressed (with the right message per publication). But at times of tight budgets, for example, you may need to make tough decisions what to focus on and which publications to consciously avoid.

Another very common procedure of measuring volume is to do a *comparison with advertising.*

This is typically done by measuring the space covered by 'your' article in square centimetres and comparing it with the amount of money it would have cost to place an advert or advertorial in this space.

Very often, high-level managers – and especially financial controllers – like this measure, since it gives them results in the language they speak: dollars. And, as a result, PR managers are often forced to make use of this criterion.

In 1999, Porter Novelli sponsored a programme of research to identify the top measurement methods used to convince PR budget holders and decision-makers. Advertising equivalents (AVEs) were considered to be one of the top five measures by clients' in-house resources.

Even so, PR professionals know that AVEs are not the most appropriate measures for PR.

Why not?

It is a fallacy to believe that the 'advertising dollar comparison' allows a direct return of investment calculation. Advertising is by definition an unfiltered message delivered by a vendor. Every vendor will praise his products in his advertising. No advertising provides a balanced opinion.

Al Ries and Laura Ries make an even more drastic statement in their recent book, *The Fall of Advertising and the Rise of PR*: '... the average consumer feels that the information presented in advertisements is one-sided. It doesn't tell the whole story, it doesn't present alternatives, and it is often misleading. No wonder advertising practitioners are only one step above car salesmen'.

An article written by an independent journalist, however, can be considered a first level of neutral reference for your message. A positive article about your company or your product is worth many advertisements. The reader expects you to say something nice about yourself in an advertisement. In an article, however, the same message is given much more weight.

So it should not be a surprise to see that the evaluations of previous tests have shown that the impact of PR supporting product introductions is more significant than other communication channels. For example, several studies have been done in the past especially for consumer products where simultaneous product introductions were carried out in several test areas. The introductions were supported by different mixes of PR and advertising per test area. As a general rule, it can be observed that the more PR work done during a product introduction, the better the results – not only in terms of output, but especially in terms of outcome of the campaign.

Again, Al Ries and Laura Ries comment on the above in a very stern way: 'Compared to the power of the press, advertising has almost zero credibility'.

In addition to not being able to indicate what impact the coverage has had on sentiment or behaviour, one of the best arguments against using an advertising equivalent as a PR measure is the following line of thought: the advertising equivalent does not take into account the value of a negative or damaging article *not* being published in the first place due to effective PR. Many PR managers have probably gone through the exercise of briefing a journalist on certain facts and then realised that his intended article was based on incorrect or only limited information. As a result, he decided in the end not to publish it at all. The effort that goes into such an activity could be quite intense, but even so the advertising equivalent would be zero and not reflect the work involved. However, the value to the company could be tremendous.

Once again a cultural aspect should be considered here. When consumers are the target of a campaign, their trust in articles in the papers may vary significantly from target audience to target audience, and also from country to country.

In order to calculate the proper value of an article, a new parameter needs to be introduced which reflects the favourability of the article from negative through neutral to positive. You may want to agree that a neutral article is worth as much as an advertisement, whereas a positive article becomes more valuable the more positive it is.

WeberShandwick has introduced a point scheme called the 'influence tracker', which is flexible and can be modified per PR campaign (see Appendix B). Using this index, an article can score between 0 and 12 points. A score of 6 is considered neutral. As a result, you may want to weigh the dollar value of an article like this:

$$V = A * I / 6$$

where

A is the value of the respective advertising amount, and
I is the achieved influence tracker value.

The above formula implies that the value of an article is up to twice the value of corresponding advertising. This factor of 2 is subject to much discussion. Sometimes it is seen to be as great as 3, sometimes it is even seen as high as 10. It is probably a waste of time to negotiate this value since it is subject to individual perception. Since the comparison with advertising has its challenges anyway, a simple comparison is probably more valuable than a sophisticated approach that is questionable overall.

The 'influence tracker' approach to measuring your results has the big advantage of being easy to use and it should be considered to be almost self-explanatory. It is therefore an ideal tool for management summaries. Its other advantage is that it can easily be tailored to any company's specific demands.

A disadvantage, however, is that it does not take into account the circulations of the publications in which the respective articles were published, nor does it specify the type of publications. It can be argued, however, that the latter should not be an issue since one must identify target publications at the planning phase of a PR campaign.

The ideal, however, is to combine the above criteria and only look at a dollar equivalent in combination with other measurement tools.

When comparing advertising with the outcome of PR one important aspect should not be overlooked. The cost associated with advertising is significantly higher than the cost associated with PR. Usually, the difference in order of magnitude in cost is estimated if you try to achieve the same impressions in PR or in advertising. While PR requires manpower, that is, time given by PR specialists – and, for example, press lunches and dinners, an advertising campaign requires not only the involvement of creative individuals, but also media planning and buying, costly production agencies and the purchase of media space. Therefore, the cost for a 'PR impression' should be considered to be in the order of a few pence, while the cost for an 'advertising impression' could easily be a few pounds. Thus, in order to do a proper calculation of the return on investment, you need to take into account the involved costs and the impact you can make with the respective outcome.

With the introduction of WeberShandwick's influence tracker we have already crossed the border between quantity and quality measurements.

Let us now have a closer look at more quality-driven criteria.

QUALITY

Two things should catch a reader's attention immediately: the headline and the use of picture material. Therefore, they are of very high importance when considering the impact 'your' article will have.

When you start to develop a PR campaign, you should have your intended *headline* already defined and your entire goal should be to get as much as possible of your desired headline finally into writing. The closer the written headline is to your preferred one the more you have succeeded.

In fact, you should define certain words that you want to appear in the final headline. These could be your company name, a certain product name, a spokes- person's name, a certain feature of your product or certain key words like 'price leader', 'aggressiveness' (against the competition), 'most reliable partner', and so on.

You should be aware that you may need to share the headline with one of your competitors if the article is comparing several companies. Ideally this should always be avoided. You obviously would not intentionally provide your competitor with some free publicity. We would argue that only in very rare cases do you want to have your competitor share the limelight, that is, the headline with you. You would probably prefer a headline like 'Company A's new product kills the previous market leader Company B' – at least as long as you are with company A...

The use of *picture or graphical material* is the second criterion you should pay great attention to. Picture material could include product photos you have made available to the media yourself, a picture of one of your spokespeople, a picture of your company's site or a diagram. You should always observe what kind of picture material is preferred by the media. If you produce your own picture material, you will soon see what was picked up and what material was not used. In your next PR campaign, this will allow you to focus even more on providing the media with exactly what they need.

One of the best examples of 'picture placement' was probably provided by Nokia. For many years, the Finnish company has been extremely effective in ensuring that in virtually any article written in Europe about mobility and in particular about mobile phones, an accompanying picture showed one of their products. They have been so dominant that customers sometimes had to ask themselves if there were actually any other vendors in the market producing mobile phones.

If, on the other hand, you depend on the journalists to take their own pictures, you should always make sure that you create sufficient photo opportunities for the journalists. This could range from just an interesting backdrop at a press conference, to your products being placed in an interesting environment, or to celebrities making use of one of your products. The options are endless.

Another criterion for evaluation is the appearance of *quotes* in an article. Quotes can be from many different sources. You may think that a good quote from one of your company spokespeople is the best that can happen to you.

Well, think again: according to Abraham Lincoln 'Nothing can be successful if public opinion is against it, and nothing will fail if public opinion will vote for it'.

The best quote you can get is a reference from one of your customers! A statement from a user of your products or services about how satisfied he is with your company is about the most convincing you can hope for.

The second best quote is a statement from an industry analyst on your product and/or your product strategy. Tracking analyst quotes also gives you a good under-standing of who the most influential analysts are in your business, that is, who you should closely work with either to learn about what is going on in the industry or to ensure that the analyst is aware of your company and its current and future offerings.

For a consumer-focused message, the involvement of a celebrity is very common practice. A quote from a celebrity can be a double-edged sword, since a lot depends on the public image of the person and the fit with your product. And, don't forget that the image of a person can change overnight.

In the business press, a positive statement from a security analyst is a valuable asset – usually even more valuable than a quote from a celebrity or an industry analyst since it has a direct impact on your share price.

Quotes from your spokespeople are still very important to get into an article, since it is a proven fact that the quality or favourability of an article increases significantly when a quote is included.

The *favourability (or rating)* of an article in itself is obviously one of the most important criterion you need to pay attention to.

A good first approach is to put articles into one of three trays. They are defined as positive, neutral and negative. This sorting already gives you a very good idea of what is thought of your company or your company's products.

A more sophisticated approach is to rate articles on a finer scale. For example, you may define a scale of 0 to 10. You rate the most negative article with a 0 and the most positive one with a 10. This type of approach is often taken when an attempt is made to describe PR performance using a certain index based on a mathematical formula (see also Appendix B). It is really important to ensure that the process used to derive the favourability is appropriate for your specific PR campaign.

For example, the person who evaluates the article should look at it with the eyes of a reader, not from your own company's perspective. In other words, you should not judge an article from within your own company, but employ some external resource to do this job – based on a proper briefing.

It is also important to take cultural differences into consideration. For example, you may judge an article written in another country in a very different way from that of native readers. It is important to note that readers in different countries may perceive one and the same article in very different ways based on their different cultural background. At one extreme: in some countries great trust is put in anything that is written in black and white, while in other countries statements in the press are automatically questioned.

Often fine nuances decide on how positive or negative an article is. The reader must be very knowledgeable of the language the article is written in. And the person must also be very familiar with the cultural environment. Therefore, the reader should be a local citizen living in the country where the article was published.

A typical example of this happening is Japan, where you will not find very many negative articles, whereas criticism is typically hidden between the lines. To the European eye, they do not seem to write any negative articles. Another example is a country that tends to have a more aggressive press than others. Norway and especially the UK are in this camp. At the other end of the spectrum, you will find countries like Germany and the Netherlands, where coverage is typically much more balanced and 'aggressive bashing' occurs only in an exceptional case.

These cultural aspects often make it very difficult to compare PR performances across countries. As we have seen, not only the size of the countries or the media landscapes have an influence, but also the perception of the attitude expressed in an article can be different from country to country. One way of calibrating your results is to always compare them with the respective competition per country. In addition, you may want to consider companies' market shares per country or company sizes as measured for example in terms of revenues.

Finally, we want to come back to the demographical aspect. If the *demographic audience* of your addressed publications is known, an analysis of your coverage can become very detailed, allowing you to identify the audiences that have been reached most or least effectively. In reality, an analysis on this level is prohibitive to many companies due to the comparatively high cost/value ratio.

DISPLAYING RESULTS

We have now seen a lot of criteria you may want to measure your PR campaign against. How do you display the results, once you have collected the data?

You can do this by making use of spreadsheets (that nobody reads...) or you can choose a graphical representation. A very typical display showing the results of a campaign is given in Figure 5.1. These diagrams are also known as 'spider-diagrams'.

In this diagram, the 'topics' are the criteria you measure your campaign against. In fact, your 'topics' could be any quality or quantity criterion. They could also be values your company wants to be seen to represent. In that case you should see a better coverage of those values that your PR campaign focused on while coverage on others stayed relatively poor.

If you are interested in the geographical distribution of your results, the 'topics' can also be regions or countries.

For each topic you enter two data points into the diagram. One has been taken before your PR campaign started, the second one afterwards. All 'before' and all 'after' data points are then connected, respectively.

For a successful campaign, the enclosed area should grow from before to after, especially in those directions that your campaign focused on.

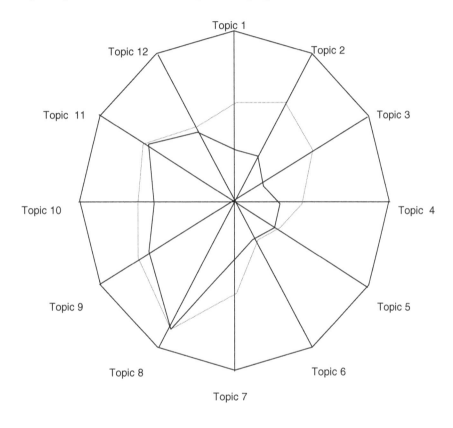

— Before the campaign
.... After the campaign

Figure 5.1 Results of a PR campaign

The case described in Figure 5.1 was based on a campaign that featured topics 1–4 where performance for those topics grew significantly, while the other topics only enjoyed minor improvements.

Figure 5.1 shows a comparatively simple example of the results of a PR campaign. Unfortunately, reality tends to be more complicated than doing such a straightforward 'before/after' comparison. The diagram does not take into account a comparison with your competitors nor does it reflect potential seasonal variations.

For example, if the criterion used in Figure 5.1 was volume of coverage, you should consider a seasonal impact, that is, you would expect for example a decrease in media coverage during the holiday season that has nothing to do with your campaign. If a seasonal aspect overlaps with your campaign, the simple 'before/after' analysis could lead you to false conclusions. In that case, a comparison with last year's data would be very valuable – if that data exists. Unfortunately, not many companies have long histories of consistent evaluation data.

A comparison of your PR performance over the same period the previous year sounds a very reasonable thing to do. However, as much as it would help to interpret your data, you still need to be very careful in simply comparing pure numbers. Several things could have changed over the past 12 months: maybe the market has changed; maybe the competitive landscape has changed; maybe some of your data is again influenced by events that are not related to the campaign you want to measure now.

Just assume for a moment that the time period you are looking at saw some significant announcements last year. This could be a special announcement of one of your competitors, a significant acquisition or merger announcement, the demise of a popular figure in the industry or an industry event, like a trade show (that is not run on an annual basis).

So, by all means, do compare the results of your PR campaign with your performance in the same time window from 12 months ago. But do some proper data mining before you judge the results of your campaign.

Example: Corporate PR and product PR

This example showcases three separate topics that are independent of one another:

•   Firstly, it shows that strategic announcements on a corporate level can indeed not only overshadow the results of more tactical product specific PR, but can also have a direct impact on them. In this case, a corporate announcement created product specific press coverage, that is, corporate PR and product PR are not independent.

•   Secondly, the example shows that an announcement can be a singular event that influences the average coverage dramatically – and would even significantly overshadow product specific PR projects that ran in parallel.

•   Finally, if you want to run another PR campaign one year after a significant announcement, you need to be aware of the fact that you cannot compare the coverage after the campaign with the coverage of the previous year, since it was not showing the standard 'background noise coverage'.

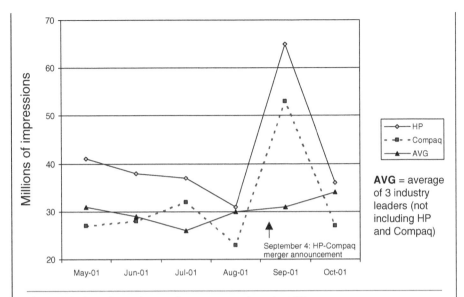

Figure 5.2 Interdependency of corporate and product PR

Figure 5.2 shows the press coverage of HP and Compaq during their merger announcement in September 2001 in EMEA. Only articles are tracked that focus on product related topics. Articles that address other aspects of the merger like economic consequences or the impact on executives are not considered in these statistics.

In September, both HP and Compaq experienced a significant increase in product specific media coverage due to the fact that the media compared both companies' product lines and started to speculate on their respective futures. At the same time, product specific coverage of other companies was almost unaffected.

It is obvious that if HP ran any PR campaign in September 2002, its results should not be compared to the companies' media results generated in the same month a year before.

INTERNAL MEASURES

Many aspects of a PR campaign can also be measured by means of internal company processes rather than 'just' being message driven. Since these processes can vary significantly from company to company, we do not want to cover them in detail but only address them generically. You may want to consider the following to be a checklist of things you may want to have a closer look into before you start to work on a new PR campaign.

- You should ensure that your PR campaign is in line with other communication campaigns that are run by the company. For example, you need to ensure that other branches in your company do not run another campaign addressing the same journalist base at the same time with an unrelated message. Also, you should ensure that your advertising or your customer communication or sponsorship programme is in line with your PR campaign. Thus, you need to ensure consistency of messaging, consistency across multiple outbound communication channels and consistency in timing.

In this context, it is worth making a comment about the publications you target for your campaign. If you run a coordinated campaign, for example, involving PR and advertising, you want to make sure that the target publications of both communication channels are aligned. There may be reasons why your advertising targets are not identical with your PR targets, but this fact should be the result of a conscious decision and not just happen by accident. In larger corporations, however, it could be that this coordination is not forthcoming. This could be as a result of PR being done in-house, while advertising is outsourced – and both teams are operating independently. A good approach then would be to look at the coordination from a measurement point of view and compare the list of publications in which you purchase advertising space with the list of target publications that you track in your PR evaluation. The learning and leverage effects for both the PR and the advertising teams could be tremendous.

- You want to ensure that you follow corporate guidelines in your company. This would include different aspects, like the use of your company logo or the selection process of supporting agencies.

- You want to ensure that the financial part of the project stays under control. The obvious goal is not to overspend on the given budget. But there may be other internal company expense rules or policies.

Finally, we would strongly recommend that you measure yourself carefully on an ongoing basis on fundamentals of your profession. You should update your basic tools regularly – just like a football forward needs to be ready at any point in time to score.
  These generic measures include the following:

- Your journalist database with all contact details is kept up-to-date on an ongoing basis.

- You maintain a contact database and/or interview database that contains all meetings between your spokespeople and press representatives. You should store information about who participated and what was discussed.

- You should maintain an internal spokespeople database that contains all certified speakers with details such as

  - Speaker's name.
  - Speaker's job title.
  - Topics the speaker can cover.
  - Ideally, a backup speaker.
  - Speaker's biography.
  - Speaker's photography.

- You need to ensure that all your company spokespeople have been certified and at least have undergone a formal or informal press training. If that is not the case, you may want to calculate the percentage of speakers who have had formal training and increase that percentage up to 100 per cent as quickly as possible.

- In case you maintain a web portal for the media (that is, a virtual press room on the Internet), you need to ensure that it is always kept up-to-date. If it is not updated regularly, it may not serve its purpose of attracting journalists to do regular checks on news from your company.

Finally, we should also measure ourselves against generic company internal processes. These become increasingly important according to the size of the company. While informal processes work very well for small and medium businesses, large organisations require more discipline. For example, service level agreements (SLAs) between the PR department and the internal stakeholders need to be documented, communicated and followed up. In order to avoid overcommunication or lack thereof, clear communication processes need to be followed. And, the planning processes should be clearly documented. In large organisations it may not be sufficient to spend half an hour with the marketing manager to define the communication strategy for the coming quarter, but a lengthy process may be required involving multiple entities and dozens of individuals. Since these processes can become very time-consuming they need to be kicked off very early. Often the planning process will then happen on two levels. On a strategic level it may need an entire year with defined time windows for certain campaigns. On the tactical level the focus is on implementation within a narrow time window of maybe only three months.

CHAPTER 6

Measuring
Long-term Trends

Get your facts first – then you can distort them as you please.
Mark Twain (1835–1910)

CONSIDERATIONS AND CRITERIA

One could argue that the true value of PR is indeed to have a long-term impact while the short-term results could be considered to be more or less tactical only. We do not want to come down on the side of one or the other, but it is without question that long-term goals should always be planned in when designing a PR campaign.

Also, it is always important to recognise that short-term results may hide a general trend. In particular, when you compare the performances of large organisations with each other, results over a short period in time could be due to multiple campaigns for each company running in parallel or they could still be due to activities which happened only briefly before the respective evaluation time window.

An additional challenge in today's industry is the fact that changes happen very quickly. New technologies emerge, new companies appear and disappear in the industrial landscape, companies reorganise, merge and spin-off at a fast pace. All these changes make it very difficult to keep long track records of consistent PR results. Very often data does not exist at all or it requires a detailed interpretation before being able to make use of it.

Speed – and time – indeed play an increasing role in evaluating PR. For example, I received my quarterly media analysis report from my evaluating agency six weeks after the end of the quarter, that is, more than four months after the start of the evaluated period. Evaluation and compiling of the results obviously takes time, but lead times of six weeks do not give you an opportunity to initiate corrective actions if anything has gone wrong.

In order to shorten lead times, many agencies have decided to offer their analysis reports online rather than compiled in a long document sent by e-mail (or even by standard mail). Online services often allow for an additional comfort factor. Not only do they provide an instant overview of what is available at any point in time, but they also allow you to customise how the data is viewed in line with your needs. For example, today you may want to zoom into the PR results of a specific country because you suspect issues there, or in a week from now you may want to get an overview of what a specific journalist has recently written in order to prepare for an upcoming interview with that particular journalist.[1]

Example: Media analysis online

In 2002/2003, Echo Research established an online analysis service for Hewlett-Packard's Imaging and Printing Group in EMEA (Europe/Middle-East/Africa). Due to legal limitations relating to copyrights in several European countries, the information kept online was not the articles themselves, but all analysis parameters relating to the articles. The online service complemented the on-going reporting services very well.

While the ongoing reports continued to provide data in a consistent way allowing for long-term trends analysis, the online service gave immediate access to customised one-time reports. This information was now available at your fingertips rather than hidden somewhere in a huge repository only being available to specialists at Echo Research.

With the online service, decision cycles were reduced significantly. A programme manager himself now had direct access to information that could play an important role in deciding to run future campaigns in this way or another.

If your company is listed on the stock exchange, one of the most sensitive measures is your company's share price. It represents shareholder value and should be the strongest indicator of the performance of the company.

Often the share price is considered to be the most important parameter by far for every company when it comes down to measuring the company on one criterion. This in itself can be subject to endless discussions that we do not want to contribute to at this point. Still, we want to comment on the fact that often PR is measured against the development of the share price.

---

1   Another way of staying ahead of the curve is a special service you may want to offer to your executives. They may not be too interested in detailed clippings generated at some point in the past (potentially even in languages they do not understand). But, they are interested in what is going on in the world or in the industry *today*. In order not to be caught catnapping, a short summary of what is in the press today is much appreciated by most executives – similar to Zazu's morning report in Disney's *Lion King*. Depending on what your resources allow, the report could cover just the headlines plus a two to three line summary of the most important articles. This could also be a more detailed document with a one-page management summary (never underestimate the power of executive summaries!) and with full article texts attached. Our own experience shows that a daily service like this highlighting the five to 20 most relevant articles for your business, derived from the top ten business titles, is ideal for most managers.

The most sophisticated service is probably the combination of a management summary and the availability of the complete clip. Companies like Xtreme provide online services that offer just that. They send out daily bulletins to an audience defined by their client. These newsletters contain two-line summaries per press article and an online link to the complete article. This is done on an international basis with articles coming from across Europe and the summaries being in English.

The share price is a result of many parameters. They include top line and bottom line performance of the company, that is, revenue, cost structure and profitability. They also include future business opportunities, subjective perception and many external influences like economic trends or industry specific ups and downs.

There should be no doubt that the effects of PR contribute to the value of the share price – and in fact that is one of the main reasons why PR is done. But these effects should not be seen in isolation. It is impossible to conclude that a certain drop in the ocean is from a certain river; equally it is impossible to relate stock price changes to a certain cause.

We can now discuss other long-term measures for PR.

The most obvious one is simply to do the basic evaluations on the outcome level, for example, the number of impressions over a longer period and observed trends. These trends could, for example, be done per country, per product range, or per industry.

One can also do a comparison of your region's performance versus the performance of your own company in other regions. And comparisons should always be done versus the competition.

When comparing with the competition, there are several recommendations of who to compare against. According to Katherine Paine (former CEO of the Delahaye Group), you should compare yourself at least against an industry leading company, a company with a similar position in the industry as yourself and against an underdog.

Assuming that your company is already one of the industry leaders, we would consider comparing your company primarily against peers in the industry. However, there are two exceptions.

The first one is the strong recommendation to pay attention to newcomers in the industry. Often the entry of a new player goes hand in hand with a lot of hype. This became only too apparent during the days of the 'Internet bubble'. All of a sudden companies were in the limelight even though they only had a handful of employees, a business idea and a budget from an optimistic investor. They enjoyed more coverage than traditional companies with proven track records.

The appearance of particular newcomers may cause a dent in your own perfor-mance curve, but you will go back to normal after only a short time. The appearance of other newcomers may again cause an initial dent in your own performance, and they are able to maintain a significant PR market share which eats into your own. This should trigger an evaluation on your side to find out what can be done to regain to your previous coverage.

The second exception is to look beyond your own industry and compare yourself with companies in other markets. This is of interest especially when it comes to criteria like brand awareness or rankings like 'best employer to work for'. Companies selling consumer products need to focus in particular on comparing themselves with players in other areas.

In several countries a lot of attention is paid to the question of how big your company's investment is inside the country. This is usually taken as an indication of

Example: Measuring against the competition

In 2000, media analysis at HP showed that the company was about head-to-head in press coverage with one of their main competitors for a certain topic. Both companies generated about the same number of articles. Both companies generated about the same favourability in the media for their respective messages. However, the competitor has been generating a significantly higher number of impressions compared to HP.

A more detailed analysis of the data showed that the competitor apparently focused their PR work on a well-defined list of high-volume publications. At HP it was understood that their messages had to be elevated to a different level in order to reach those publications. This included an integrated message across different product ranges and articulation of the message in a way that made it relevant for the business press.

The following figure proves that the PR managers at HP have indeed been able to learn from the results of their media analysis. The implementation of the learning resulted in the following development of the impressions per article that were generated in the following business quarters.

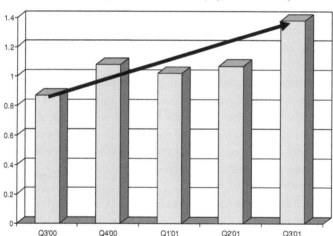

(Impressions/article) vendor 1 relative to (impressions/article) vendor 2

Figure 6.1 Impressions per article

The number of articles and the impression value varied significantly over time. In order to take this seasonality out of the equation, the above diagram shows the relative performance of both companies – the performance is measured in 'impressions divided by number of articles' where a result smaller than 1 means that one company is better, a value greater than 1 means the other one is better.

how committed the company is to the local market. In this case, you are compared with companies that operate in very different fields – whether you want it or not. And, as a result you need to be prepared to address this topic as part of your PR work. So, your measures should also reflect these facts.

Before we move on, here is a list of typical values that should be looked at in a long-term trend analysis:

- Number of articles

- Number of articles per publication

- Tone (or sentiment or favourablity rating)

- 'Slugging average'

- Prominence

- Calibrated volume (company size versus share of voice)

- Corporate/brand/product tracking

- Spokespeople

- Headlines

- Industry topics

- Industry analyst quotes.

We will now go through these criteria one by one:

NUMBER OF ARTICLES

It is sometimes difficult to keep the base of your measurements the same. For example, certain publications may disappear from the market, others may appear. Budget constraints may require you to limit the number of evaluated publications over certain periods. Be aware of these changes when you derive your conclusions from the raw data.

NUMBER OF ARTICLES PER PUBLICATION

This value is often looked at in order to estimate the absolute number of evaluated publications required. If you measure yourself against the number of articles per publication – and not against the number of articles itself – the publications themselves can theoretically change from one measurement to the next. However, you will still see an impact if you look at aspects like the type of publications (daily newspapers, business press, trade press, for example) and their frequency. On average you should expect fewer articles in publications that appear on a monthly basis compared to publications issued on a weekly basis.

You should certainly note which publication covers you most and know which publications pay attention to your company more than other companies. In the same way, you should check to see if your competitors have 'home bases', that is, if certain publications are leaning strongly towards your competitors. These publications may be specific targets for upcoming PR campaigns.

TONE (OR SENTIMENT OR FAVOURABILITY RATING)

Every written article can be attributed a certain value describing the tone of it. Scales may vary from system to system, but, in general, an article is either characterised as positive, neutral or negative. Most commonly, scales run from 0 to 100 (50 being neutral), or from –5 to +5 (0 being neutral).

It should be noted that this way of describing the tone of an article does not tell you anything about the significance of it! You may have generated a beautiful article praising your company to be the best invention since sliced bread – but it was published in a low-circulation paper not read by your customer base. At the same time, the *Wall Street Journal* may have published a very damaging article about your company. While it seems that both articles average out to neutral coverage, you will soon begin to realise the – in this case sad – truth.

'SLUGGING AVERAGE'

The slugging average (SA) is a comparatively simple measure for the quality or rating of press coverage. It is based on the comparison of positive/neutral articles on a certain topic with the negative articles on the same topic:

SA = number of positive and neutral articles / number of negative articles.

Thus, an SA of, for example, 25 means that for every 25 positive or neutral articles one negative article is written.

The big advantage of using the SA to measure rating is its simplicity. It is easy to use when setting a certain goal for your PR work and it is easy to measure.

On the other hand, the simplicity also leads to its downfall. The SA does not tell you anything about the reach of the articles, that is, it does not tell you anything about the impact of the articles. A negative article on the front page of a very influential magazine obviously has a much stronger impact than a (short) negative article on page 16 in a low-volume publication which maybe does not even address your target audience.

So, the results can be very misleading. However, we should realise that a normal favourability rating (not taking into account the publications' reaches) suffers from the same drawbacks. In fact, a normal favourability rating (usually given in percentage) also has the disadvantage of being misleading for a different reason. A favourability of 80 per cent, for example, may still look very positive. The 80 per cent translates into an SA of four, however. And the picture is not so rosy anymore once you understand that for every four 'good' articles, one negative article was written. In that respect, the SA is much more brutal.

Another negative aspect of the slugging average is that it takes a binary approach to the value of an article. It is either in the 'good' bin, that is, positive or neutral, or it is in the 'bad' bin, that is, the article is considered to be negative. The slugging average does not differentiate between positive and neutral coverage.

Figure 6.2 translates the favourability or tone into SA values.

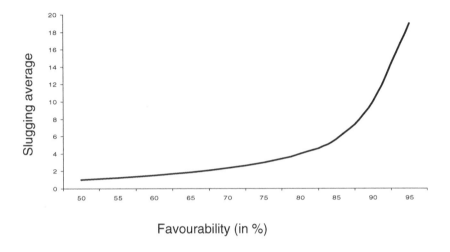

Figure 6.2   Favourability vs. 'slugging average'

It becomes obvious that – due to the finer detail of the scale – the SA allows clearer differentiation than when using favourability when your coverage is fairly positive (90 per cent or above). However, favourability allows clearer differentiation when you go through a crisis situation with poor press coverage.

PROMINENCE

An article delivered to you by a clipping service could cover your company or its products in many ways. It could be a feature article dedicated to your company or its products or you are only briefly mentioned – either as one among many other companies or in an article leading with news from one of your competitors.

In fact, we should consider prominence to be the third most important dimension in media analysis after volume (as measured by number of articles) and quality (as measured in tone). In typical measurement indices, prominence is either a single parameter that takes into account many aspects like placement, an evaluation of the headline, and so on, or it is indirectly present through a collection of parameters like the focus of the article, presence of quotes from spokespeople, and so on. In Appendix B you will see examples of both approaches.

CALIBRATED VOLUME (COMPANY SIZE VERSUS SHARE OF VOICE)

As we have already seen in the previous chapter, it is often necessary to calibrate your results when comparing your own PR results against the competition. We have seen that this is true when comparing results across different regions. In the context of a trend analysis, we need to ensure that we do not compare apples with oranges when we compare our company's share of voice with that of a significantly larger or a significantly smaller competitor.

There are several ways of calibrating share of voice against company size. The obvious one is integrated into Delahaye's Media Reputation Index (MRi) – see Appendix B. It is based on taking the revenue of a company as a measure of company size.

If a company is present only in a single market, a comparison versus market share figures as provided by industry analysts is also a good reference. Comparing share of voice with market share figures may also be done if volume (number of articles) is looked at for individual product lines of a larger corporation.

CORPORATE/BRAND/PRODUCT TRACKING

Coverage which you generate can be on different levels and can contain different content. You may see articles that discuss your company on a corporate level. You may see articles that discuss your company brands or sub-brands (if your company brand is considered your main brand). Or you may see articles that discuss your company's products and their features.

It is obvious that you cannot compare these articles with one another nor can you compare them versus the same competitive articles. So, simply adding them up to show a high number of generated articles is the wrong approach.

At the same time, your product groups are interested in the results by product and other internal stakeholders in your PR department are interested in brand coverage.

So, depending on your company size and structure, you should track product coverage, brand coverage and corporate coverage separately.

SPOKESPEOPLE

Check how spokespeople are covered in the press. Compare your own speakers with key speakers from the competition. You may also want to compare if the right speakers get visibility in the press or if important messages are overshadowed by very dynamic speakers who cover less important topics.

HEADLINES

Headlines can be evaluated by volume share per vendor and are also related to the rating of the headlines. Just looking at the sheer volume could be misleading because most headlines may be negative.

INDUSTRY TOPICS

In order to find out what is currently hot in your industry you want to find out what topics are getting most coverage. You can do this by looking into the articles written per topic across all vendors, but also by individual competitor. The latter could actually provide support for your business intelligence, since it should give you some idea what the focus and intentions of your respective competitors are.

If you are responsible for multiple product lines, you should measure articles per topic rather than looking at the overall picture. Also, you should compare with competitors then by topic, because competition may vary per product or message. You should find out what your leading products are and what the rating is per product or product line. You may identify a product range that might be considered to be your secret weapon for getting press coverage or TV or radio airtime.

Let us look at an example: the topic 'mobile/wireless' has been a widely covered topic in the IT industry for several years. Your company may provide a wide range of IT solutions, some of them addressing the area of mobility. Overall, you may experience satisfying coverage of your company and its offerings. But, an analysis of the coverage for mobility solutions in the market may reveal that you are significantly outperformed in that area by the competition. You now see this finding as an opportunity to gain more visibility for your company by focusing your PR activities on your mobility solutions in order to increase your overall media coverage.[2]

INDUSTRY ANALYST QUOTES

There are several reasons why you want to have a very close look into industry analyst quotes. You will find out who the most quoted analysts, that is, leading influencers, are. You will also learn about their attitude towards the various vendors. And, you will learn something about the relations between certain journalists and certain analysts. Based on that knowledge you can align your outreach to those analysts and journalists.

DISPLAYING RESULTS

A very good overview of trends in your PR results can be given in a two-dimensional diagram that has a quantity measure on one axis (for example, the number of generated articles) and a quality measure on the other (for example, a quality rating).

---

2   In this context it is interesting to note that there are certain similarities between using industry topics as a segmentation to identify PR opportunities and the identification of company values to increase PR coverage for your company.
     It is common practice to explore which values are connected to which companies in the industry. Some values are clearly connected to certain companies, some values are not really owned by any company. If these values match with your company's goals and strategies, you may want to adopt (one of) them and run strong branding campaigns to position your company accordingly.

Your PR performance will fall into one of the following quadrants:

1.   You enjoy positive coverage, but the number of publications which are inter-
     ested in covering your company is low, that is, the number of articles you
     generate is low. This scenario is typical for a promising startup company. It
     is not yet widely recognised, but its innovative products or business model
     causes journalists to write positive articles. We call this quadrant 'spring'.

2.   Once your company becomes more popular while it continues to thrive in
     the industry, the volume goes up. You have reached the stage we call
     'summer'.

3.   The third quadrant is characterised by high volume and a low quality
     rating. This stage is a typical crisis situation requiring urgent correction, or
     your company can consider itself to be in the 'autumn' of its life.

4.   Finally, the fourth quadrant can be considered 'winter': hardly any coverage,
     and if there is any, then it is negative. This is a typical scenario for a company
     that nobody pays attention to anymore – a company that is either operating
     in a downward spiral, or a new company that is off to a bad start.

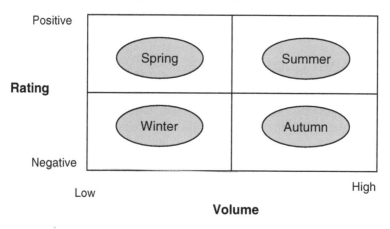

Figure 6.3 Quality/quantity diagram

Just as in real life, we are looking for an endless summer in PR. Unlike in real life,
however, the sequence of the seasons is not defined. For example, you can move from
summer to spring, that is, you continue to enjoy positive coverage, but the volume goes
down. Also, an escalation of a crisis situation can move you from winter to autumn.

Now, it is interesting to follow your path in the 'season-diagram' over time. Figure
6.4 shows an example with four data points representing the PR performance of four
consecutive quarters. The diagram can indeed be considered to be the highest-level
overview of your company's PR department's performance.

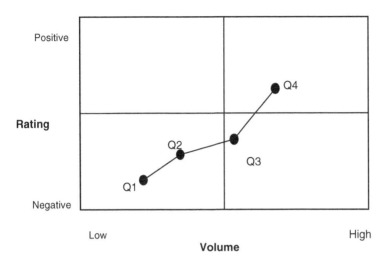

Figure 6.4   PR performance over time

A diagram similar to Figures 6.3 or 6.4 is used by several PR agencies to provide their clients with a quick snapshot overview of their performance. The quality is often measured by using a favourability rating and the quantity is typically measured using the achieved circulation or the number of impressions (see Chapter 5).

For example, PR media intelligence companies like the Observer Group or Report International provide results in graphics like Figure 6.4 and 6.5.

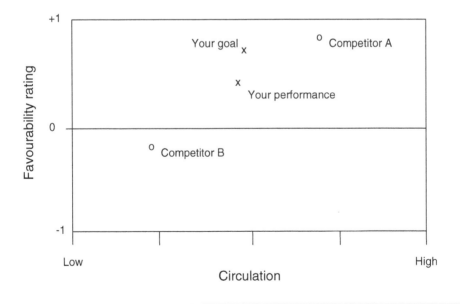

Figure 6.5   Favourability/circulation diagram

It should be stressed again that favourability and circulation are independent parameters. You can experience a favourability that is better than your competitor's yet you may reach a smaller audience, or vice versa.

The diagram also allows you to compare actual achievements with targeted goals. So, at one glance, as in Figure 6.5, you can compare your achievements with your competition and with your own ambitions.

Another example shows, how powerful the visualisation 'favourability-over-circulation' actually is. You may want to split your overall performance by looking into certain subjects like products, product features, markets, brands, company values, geographical regions, etc. The diagram would then look like this:

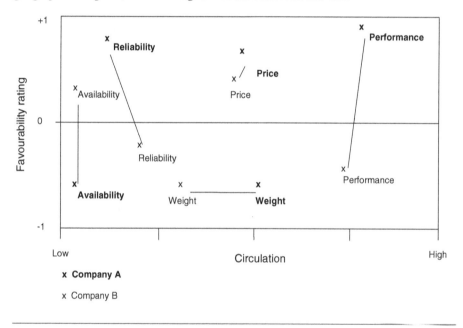

Figure 6.6 Favourability/circulation diagram (by subject)

You can now compare yourself with the competition subject by subject. For example, you may learn that you are perceived to have good prices, but you can improve on reliability. Or the products from your product division A receive more coverage than those from division B. Or your company gets a high favourability for corporate ethical standards, but scores low on innovativeness. You can slice and dice your data according to your specific needs.

It cannot be stressed enough that a complete picture of your performance can only be painted by adding the performance of your competitors to the diagram. This addition puts your performance into context, since you may now be able to explain some of the trends you observed in your own PR performance in a more objective way.

For example, without looking at your competitors' performance, you may attribute a peak in a certain quarter to a certain PR campaign you ran. A dent in your competitors' performance in the same period may support that idea. A simultaneous peak for all your competitors, however, may hint that your own peak was only due to a certain seasonal factor or due to a generic industry topic that caught the media's attention in that period.

The quality/quantity diagram can indeed be used to study several aspects of your long-term PR trends. We have just seen a few examples of these which look at trends, messages or comparison with competitors. The usage can be manifold and would always depend on the specific question you need to answer.

A final example may give you some ideas of how you want to make use of this tool in your specific case.

Assume you work for a company that tries to find out if it reaches all media types in a similar way. The company addresses trade press, business press, distribution channel press, media which address two selected vertical industries (for example, automotive and telecom) and selected consumer press segments like lifestyle and travel media.

Sorting the results of a media analysis would give the results seen in Figure 6.7:

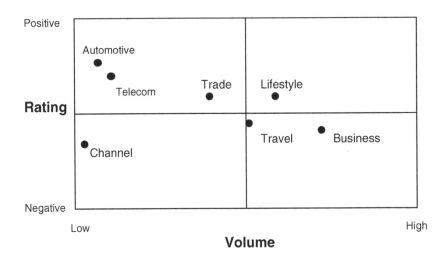

Figure 6.7 Quality/quantity diagram (by target media)

This diagram should give you a lot of food for thought that would ultimately impact significantly on your future PR activities. These may or may not include:

- The highest volume is generated by the business press. Unfortunately, they do not write very positively about your company. You may want to focus on changing that as a top priority.

- The low volume of the channel press output could be explained by the fact that not many of these publications exist (and in some cases, volume is measured in impressions, their circulation is typically comparatively low).

The fact that they write negatively about you obviously leaves a negative impression on your channel partners – especially if they write more positively about your competition at the same time. If you are very dependent on channel partners you need to correct that impression as soon as possible.

- You may want to find out why you are successful with the lifestyle press, while the travel press does not seem to favour your messages. Hopefully you can apply your positive experience with the lifestyle press to improving the coverage in the travel press.

(Example: Your company manufactures notebooks. Your messages focus on gadgets: the style and picture material which you provide to the media show the products in typical home environments. This means lifestyle media would most likely pick up these materials, whereas travel magazines would have liked you to focus maybe on product robustness, weight, battery life or even topics like the availability of an international power plug adaptor. Also, they would prefer to receive pictures of the products being used on the road. So, as a conclusion, you may want to provide a dedicated set of deliverables for the travel media, addressing their target audience.)

PR evaluation agencies including Mantra International provide analysis as in the following example.

It should be noted that there is a second possible interpretation of the quality/quantity diagram. You may, for example, want to define a parameter for your overall PR performance that is derived from multiplying a quality measure with a quantity measure, like:

*(PR performance) = (PR quantity) * (PR quality).*

The parameter 'PR performance' would then be visualised by the size of the rectangle defined by the values of 'PR quantity' and 'PR quality'. In other words: the bigger the rectangle, the better your PR performance, as can be seen in Figure 6.8.

Figure 6.8 should be a straightforward case, since in this comparison the second overall PR performance is definitely better than the first one, given that not only was a better volume achieved, but also a better quality rating.

It becomes more challenging to compare a 'high volume/low quality case' with a 'low volume/high quality case'. In other words, you need to answer the question of which parameters for quality and quantity, respectively, describe your PR goals best.

CARMA International (with support from the University of Massachusetts School of Management) has defined the 'Media IQ' (IQ = Impact – Quality Measure) as a generic single unit of measure for media coverage. It is based on the audience reach in terms of number of impressions and on CARMA's favourability rating system and is defined as

*Media IQ = Impact (audience reach) * Quality (favourability measure).*

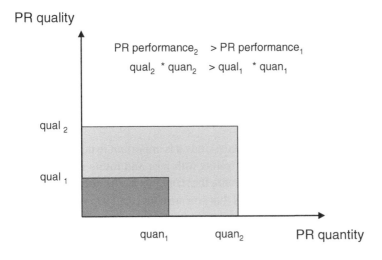

PR quality

PR performance$_2$ > PR performance$_1$

qual$_2$ * quan$_2$ > qual$_1$ * quan$_1$

qual $_2$

qual $_1$

quan$_1$ quan$_2$ PR quantity

Figure 6.8 PR performance area

Still, the question remains of whether indeed a single parameter is sufficient to describe the overall PR performance or if volume and quality ratings need to be addressed separately. We would indeed like to encourage you to work with two parameters, since volume cannot make up for a bad quality rating nor can quality coverage make up for low reach. You may in fact compare the system with your car requiring petrol *and* oil – and you cannot make up for the absence of one of the two by adding more of the other.

Until now we have focused on long-term analysis of the more traditional PR evaluations. In order to gain long-term results, very different techniques will need to be applied. They include surveys like awareness and preference studies. These studies would no longer be part of Lindenmann's output level, but fall into the outgrowths or even outcomes departments, depending on the questions asked in the survey and the conclusions that can be drawn from them.

Awareness and preference studies are based on interviews with a representative sample of your identified target audience. These studies can become quite costly. Therefore, the smaller your company is the less likely it is that you will do them.

But once you have made a decision to run a survey, you need to plan it well in advance. A survey is extremely sensitive to the manner in which it is conducted and to the questions asked.

A very typical approach is to run a survey before and after a certain activity has been executed. If you have the luxury of being able to sell your products in a test market before you enter the entire market, you almost certainly want to find out what has worked and what has not. And, most importantly, you want to be able to draw conclusions about your general performance from your test run. This means that your results can be transferred to all the regions where you ultimately want to launch your product.

Another typical area where a survey is used is during the determination of your brand awareness and preference. You can consider using this evaluation to measure the total impact your company has on your target audience, that is, your potential customers. Thus, again, not only does PR contribute to the respective results, but also to advertising, go-to-market strategies and any other appearance of your company in the public eye.

When doing an awareness and preference study it is important to take into account that you want to be able to compare the results with past and future measurements. Therefore, you should develop a questionnaire that contains all the questions that you would have asked quite some time ago and that you are convinced you would ask again in the near future. 'Quite some time ago' and 'near future' depend on the pace of your industry.

Two more criteria need to be discussed in this context.

The first one is very common if your customer is a consumer, and not a business. Especially in the entertainment industry (movies, games, music, etc) it is common practice today to keep an eye on what is discussed in online chat rooms or what is posted on newsgroups. Here you have peoples' opinion unfiltered, you hear the feedback to your PR campaigns and the long-term trends in opinion direct from the horse's mouth.

Be very careful, though, if you draw conclusions from individual opinions or from only small samples! This could quickly lead you to incorrect conclusions. However, the number of contributions posted gives you a strong indication of how your messages were received by your target audience. And the tone of the contributions can be measured in a similar way to the tone of articles published by professional journalists.

The second criterion we briefly want to mention is the attitude you create in your target audience towards the messages from your competition. In this context, target audience could again stand for your customers or the journalists. You are in an ideal position, if you have been able to make your target audience immune to your competitors' PR activities. In particular, you can be proud of your work, if you have equipped journalists with the right questions to ask your competition – questions you know they will have problems answering. When journalists react this way you have generated the highest level of loyalty in them. You have vaccinated them against all FUD[3] spread by your competitors.

It is very difficult to put this achievement into numbers and diagrams since it can be very subjective. But, you can consider it has provided you with an additional data point to position a journalist in the 'journalist's trust' diagram in Figure 4.3 discussed in Chapter 4. Nevertheless, this behaviour is probably the best indication of a positive attitude change of your audience; the change being in your favour!

---

3   FUD = Fear, Uncertainty, Doubt

CHAPTER 7

Measuring the Results of a Crisis Situation

There can't be a crisis next week. My schedule is already full.
Henry Kissinger (born 1923)

Crisis situations are very annoying. The problem is, most of them you cannot predict. They can happen at any point in time – but they should never hit you unprepared in PR! You are not expected to be prepared with an answer to solve a sudden crisis situation immediately, but you must have all the processes in place to address the issue.

First, a quick question: What is a business crisis situation in the current context?

A crisis could be anything that is of potential harm to your company's image, its brand, its people, or its business. In the context of communication, crisis PR can be defined as a special discipline where you basically have the opposite goal of 'normal PR': you want to avoid or minimise coverage in the media.

Typical examples of business crisis situations include the following:

- An accident has happened that involved one of your products. In particular, aerospace or railroad companies should be prepared to manage this type of PR situation.

- One of your products showed a defect and your company has to recall units that have already been shipped. In the case of, for example, car or computer manufacturers this could cause a recall of a large number of products and trigger significant press interest.

- The famous Y2k bug was a crisis situation in the IT world that involved more or less the entire industry.

- A lawsuit that is filed against your company could cause a crisis situation that requires you to react.

- The public have become aware of one of your employees' business mis-conducts.

- Negative rumours (regardless if true or false) about your company are spreading from unknown sources.

- Your company has to downsize, that is, you have to lay off employees.

- Your employees are on strike.

- Leak of company confidential information.

- Your company has lost a significant customer whose name is well recognised in the industry.

- Danger of bankruptcy.

- Natural or man-made disasters, kidnapping, and so on.

This book is not supposed to be a training handbook on how to manage crisis situations in PR. But some very basic rules apply to most, if not all, crisis situations.

- You want to be in control of what is said and written.

- You want to be as open with the media as possible. You do not want to come across as trying to hide relevant information from the public. Not making a comment is almost as bad as making a negative comment, and it can have a very damaging effect in certain situations. You should always remember the famous words of Paul Watzlawick:

  You cannot not communicate.

  So, crisis communication does not mean that you hide from the public. In fact, it can mean exactly the opposite in certain cases, since you want to avoid the spread of unfounded speculation.

- You want to minimise the negative coverage as much as possible – or, if you can, you may want to avoid any coverage.

In order to achieve these goals, you should have resources and processes in place that were already defined proactively. They include:

- Definition of spokespeople who are trained to comment on challenging issues.

- A core team of people who are required to manage the situation. This team should be as small as possible.

- Empowerment of the team members to make critical decisions.

- Defined communication and approval processes.

- Be careful when separating communication flow and information given to partners, customers and press.

It is very difficult to define generic measures for the success of PR during crisis situations, since all situations tend to be different – and because there is no PR plan in place that you can measure yourself against. Also, a lot depends on the point at which PR gets involved in the situation. The late involvement of PR resources can cause a situation where all the damage is already done.

We would therefore identify generic goals first that should be usable for most crisis situations.

First, some internal measurements:

- The number of people involved in the communication is to be kept to a minimum (minimum: one communications' focal point, one PR resource, one spokesperson, one legal resource, if required). Only certified speakers are allowed to talk to the press. Non-certified speakers should understand the process of who to refer to in case they are approached by the media and asked for a statement.

- Response time to media enquiries.

- Drawer statements or talking points are available at least for the most likely questions asked.

From the above you can derive several generic external measures:

- No article must appear which contains a quote from a non-certified speaker from your company.

- You need to check if you can turn the tone of the coverage around. For example, a quality issue with one of your products could result in coverage questioning the quality of all your company's products. It could also result in coverage of your company's caring attitude to its customers by proactively informing them about issues and offering them appropriate solutions.

- All external announcements need to be very carefully checked with your legal department.

- You need to have information available on how your business partners and customers comment on the situation publicly, if at all.

PREDICTABLE CRISIS SITUATIONS

A true crisis situation is usually caused by something that is not directly under your control. Therefore, any preparations cannot be focused, but can only be generic.

However, there are also crisis situations that are more or less predictable and you can make specific preparations to counter them. In many cases you can even prepare a PR plan to address foreseeable issues.

It is obvious that many of these issues are caused by internal challenges, like for example, quality issues with your products that are discovered by your quality department – even before the public becomes aware of the issues. Another example is a financial shortfall. In that case the development of a communication strategy and the processes of solving the problem should happen in parallel. If time allows, even a proper PR plan with defined goals and measures can be compiled.

A communication strategy covering such issues should address several needs, including the following:

- Communicate to all parties involved (for example, customers, media, distribution channel partners, business partners, and so on) on time and in the right order.

- Tailor messages to respective audiences to avoid any confusion or misunderstanding.

- Stay in control of the communication.

- Ensure that all communication to all audiences (customers, media, partners, and so on) is consistent in the context as well as in time.

- A consistent message is used in all communication with the media.

Most importantly, though, you need to set clear objectives for your communication. Your measures are then derived directly from those objectives.

Typically, the measures for crisis communication are much more quality driven than quantity driven. There are two reasons for that:

1. In most cases you do not want any coverage at all.

2. You want the facts to go along with your messages.

In the case of a product quality issue, this, for example, means that you want to point out that your company is committed to quality and customer value. You may want to discuss your quality measures and your track record and hopefully find them to be in your favour.

In the case of poor financial results you may want to explain the reasons behind this. Maybe your company invested in the future through a reorganisation that interrupted the business briefly. Maybe the results can be explained by a weak economy rather than by issues in your company. Maybe you had one time write-offs like payments for an acquisition or costs related to product recalls.

Whatever the case you want your explanations to be covered in the media rather than speculation or even negative comments spread by your competitors. Unfounded speculations are the worst case that can happen to you. One of the most important goals should therefore be not to even let them start – or counter them as quickly as possible.

CRISIS SITUATIONS THAT CAN BE ANTICIPATED

Several crisis situations cannot be fully predictable. They are not under your control; but they can still be anticipated.

An example of such a crisis is where one of your competitors announces a superior product to your own. In fast moving industries like, for example, the IT industry or the telecom industry, it is a common event for companies to 'leap-frog' one another. It should therefore not be a surprise when your competitor all of a sudden announces a superior mobile phone, a new service or a faster processor. Your own company is probably already working on an even better phone, an even better service or an even faster processor. Your competitor has just been a bit faster to get to market.

Since this scenario is commonplace in comparatively young industries, you can be prepared for it. It is often even common practice to have a contingency plan ready with which to address this scenario. You have several PR tools ready to address this need. It is important, though, that you do not allow your competitor to stand in the limelight alone. Instead, you need to share some of the glory – and coverage. Again, there are several ways to achieve this, for instance, by offering previews of your own developments, or by offering interviews with your own executives to put things into context.

In an ideal world, though, you should be able to build on the good PR work you have supposedly done in the past. If you have been able to position your own company as an industry leader and if you have established good relationships with key reporters the likelihood is very high that they will be proactive and approach you to provide them with a second opinion on your competitor's move. The business press, in particular, often follow this scenario.

Regardless of how you manage to get your angle of the story into press articles, a key measure should be that the story is actually present in the first place. We have already discussed throughout this book how important it is to watch the competition and compare your PR results with the results of other players in your market. Here we have a perfect example of where it pays off to pay attention to your competitors' PR activities and you may even benefit from their efforts. Giving your competitor a free ride would mean that there is room for improvement in your PR department.

You may even want to look at this issue from another angle. Assume you are the market leader in a certain industry and you let a competitor take centre stage introducing a more superior product or service to your own and you stay quiet. This could be interpreted as losing your position or even admitting your competitor's superiority. You should not allow that to happen and should take action accordingly.

However, you should only adopt this practice in a reasonable manner. For example, if you comment on every little move of your competitor, your comments could easily be perceived as FUD (Fear, Uncertainty, Doubt) against them. A decision on what to do can only be achieved in cooperation with your marketing and business colleagues.

CRISIS 'OUT OF THE BLUE'

We said earlier that there are crisis situations that you cannot make specific preparations for. Still, you can set up the processes that you would want to follow in such a situation. The investment into such planning can be compared to making regular insurance payments. You hope you will never have to make use of the insurance, but you are willing to make the regular payments.

So, in this instance you would prepare a skeleton PR plan for a crisis situation. A specific situation analysis and project description can obviously not be part of that generic plan. However, some generic processes, objectives and measures should be included.

Since many of the issues we refer to in this sub-chapter are of a relatively un-anticipated nature, there is a strong likelihood that you will only come to know of them once an article has already been published. In that case your main goal should be to control the news from spreading. Especially in the age of the Internet it is possible for some topics to spread like wildfire – even across country and language borders.[1]

The tactics that need to be used when reacting to certain bad news is always dependent on the individual case. Sometimes it is best to get strongly involved and have your own story heard. Sometimes it is advisable, though, not to get involved, even though the facts are reported incorrectly. Commenting on the story may not necessarily improve the situation for your company, but may even keep it in the spotlight for longer than necessary.

It should be noted that we are talking about a wide range of potential issues. The spectrum ranges from minor issues all the way to issues that can be seriously damaging to your business. Some of these issues may not be addressed by the PR department at all, but the company's legal and/or security department take ownership. In that case there is obviously no measure that needs to be implemented for PR.

We are fully aware that given the dynamics of journalism it is easy to request no coverage and try to limit and even avoid news being spread. But to achieve this is an art. Still, it should always be one of your top goals – and also one of the most important measures.

PR AS A PROACTIVE TOOL IN 'ISSUES COMMUNICATION'

A special case of crisis PR is the proactive commenting on upcoming issues. A typical example is a public discussion about the introduction of special regulations that would have an impact on your industry and on your company in particular.

1　The availability of the Internet has increased circulation of news significantly. The impact, especially in the context of crisis PR, should not be underestimated. While some measures are similar to the print press (like number of articles, rating, favourability, tone, and so on) others cannot be measured in exactly the same way. Criteria like impressions or advertising equivalent, for example, cannot be directly applied to Internet coverage.

You certainly want to make sure that your standpoint is heard in this discussion. This discipline in PR can almost be considered to be lobbying. However, it is not an attempt to influence decision makers directly, but it is an attempt to educate the public.

Your measurement criteria should therefore include line items like 'visibility of your standpoint versus other opinions'. This could be expressed in number of articles published, in impressions or the best option, an independent opinion poll.

Example Press Questionnaire

This questionnaire is designed to gather your views of this press event. It will help us to find out more about your needs and ensure that future events meet your requirements. Please be honest when completing this questionnaire.

Please give marks out of ten for each of the following: (1 = poor, 10 = excellent)

Morning Presentation

	Speaker 1 Title of speaker 1	Speaker 2 Title of speaker 2
Quality of the presentation:		
The value of the information given:		
The quality of the press material:		
The news value of the briefing:		

Break Out Sessions

	Topic 1	Topic 2	Topic 3	Topic 4
Quality of the presentation:				
The value of the information given:				
The news value of the briefing:				

What were the three key points you took from the event?

1. . . . .

2. . . . .

3. . . . .

How could this event have been improved for you?

. . . .

. . . .

. . . .

Overall Event: Please tick:

How would you rate the information value of this event?	1. ❏ unacceptable	2. ❏ acceptable	3. ❏ good	4. ❏ very good	5. ❏ excellent
Did the trip meet your expectations?	1. ❏ unacceptable	2. ❏ acceptable	3. ❏ good	4. ❏ very good	5. ❏ excellent
Overall, do you feel that the trip was worthwhile for you?	1. ❏ unacceptable	2. ❏ acceptable	3. ❏ good	4. ❏ very good	5. ❏ excellent
How would you rate your overall satisfaction with the event?	1. ❏ unacceptable	2. ❏ acceptable	3. ❏ good	4. ❏ very good	5. ❏ excellent

What suggestions would you make to the organisers?

. . . .

. . . .

. . . .

Name: . . . .

Publication represented: . . . .

Country: . . . .

Example Measurement Indices

In August 2001, Delahaye Medialink and the Reputation Institute announced the introduction of the Media Reputation Index (MRi). This index benchmarks corporations tracking their media coverage and its impact on corporate reputation. The mathematical details behind this index are very complex; however, the basic idea behind it is to evaluate volume of coverage and quality with a special focus on reputational drivers. Two parameters are taken into consideration to generate the MRi value. The first one is called 'prominence'. It considers aspects including placement, evaluation of headlines, use of graphics and others. The second one considers the average tone of the respective articles. The weighed result is then per article multiplied by the number of impressions, where no multipliers like, for example, number of readers per copy (see also pages 58–9), are considered. Thus, the formula for the 'net effect' defining the MRi value per corporation would be:

Net effect = S $(M_{1i}$ x $M_{2i})$ * M_{3i}
when
i: number of article
M_1: 'prominence'
M_2: tone (on a scale from 1 to 5)
M_3: impression

The net effect can be either positive or negative corresponding to a positive or negative impact of the coverage. The MRi value itself is then calculated using the following:

MRi = 100 * net effect / median net effect

This value can then be compared across corporations. You can also adjust the value to compare companies of different sizes. This would require gauging all values measuring size in terms of company revenues. The size-adjusted MRi value would then be:

$MRi_{size-adjusted}$ = 100 * (net effect/revenue) / (median net effect/median revenue)

The measurement of the MRi is a very sophisticated process that is primarily designed to compare larger corporations with one another. For more frequent use you may want to develop your own rating or you want to make use of one of the many available ratings that have been developed before, primarily by PR agencies. Below are two examples for your consideration. The first rating is based on defined multipliers per considered aspect, the second one is based on a points scheme.

- Rating of an article according to the Russian PR agency Publicity PR[2]:

  rating $= A_1{}^*A_2{}^*A_3{}^*A_4{}^*A_5{}^*A_6{}^*A_7/N$

  A_1: Number of pre-defined criteria met by the article (max =8), e.g. the inclusion of graphics or quoted spokesperson,

  A_2: Favourability of the article (2=favourable, 1=neutral, -1=negative)

  A_3: Size of the article in multiples of an A4 page

  A_4: Probability of information recall (depends on amount of information about particular company in the entire article - max is 2, or the value is 1/N, N being the number of competitors mentioned in the article)

  A_5: Circulation (in units of 100,000 - in Russia)

  A_6: Match of the theme and style of the article to the target audience of the publication (value is .5 if no match or 1 if match)

  A_7: Factor describing the repetitiveness of the generated message in multiple articles as part of a PR campaign (value is 1, if the article is a stand-alone article, or 2, if the same generated message is repeated in at least 3 articles)

  N: Number of mentioned competitors in the article (including the company itself).

- 'Influence tracker' according to the PR agency WeberShandwick:

  rating $= B_1 + B_2 + B_3 + B_4 + B_5 + B_6 (+B_7)$

  B_1: Location of coverage (value is 1, if the article appeared in pre-defined key publication, otherwise the value is 0)

  B_2: Focus of the article (value is 3, if the article does focus on your own company as the only vendor, or value is 2, if less than 30% is on your own company)

  B_3: Size of the article (value is 2, if the article is at least one quarter of a page, otherwise it is 1)

  B_4: Use of images (value is 2, if a photograph or graphic is used, otherwise it is 0)

  B_5: Spokesperson (value is 1, if a spokesperson is quoted, otherwise it is 0)

  B_6: Coverage of pre-defined key messages (value is 1 per message, maximum is 3)

  (The avoidance of potential pre-defined negative issues, maximum 3, can score points as well, if that is defined as a PR goal. The optional factor B7 is 1 per avoided negative issue.)

  The rating can therefore be between 0 and 12 with 6 being considered a neutral or fair coverage.

---

2   From: 'The role of rating in the PR activity', E. Bahareva, *Marketing*, 1 2000, ISSN 1028-5849.

APPENDIX C

Measuring Product Reviews and Awards

For some companies, the most important coverage for their products is the results of product benchmarks carried out by either the publication's test labs or even by independent test organisations. In some countries, like Germany, the results of product tests influence buyers' behaviour quite significantly.

By the way, the importance of product test results providing a benchmark is different from country to country, since buyers' behaviour differs significantly. However, there is a trend in the industry to turn even top of the range products into commodities. The more this trend continues, the more benchmarks from product tests in the media become important for customers to select the right product for their individual needs. Also, because of this trend, more and more technologies that were previously only available for business use, are now also becoming available to consumers who are looking for help to find the right tool for their specific requirements.

We have seen up to 20 per cent of the overall media coverage for certain product categories to be derived from product evaluations. There are several groups of articles separated by purpose and type of evaluation:

1. 'First look' reviews
    These reviews focus on a single product only. They are published in the timeframe when the specific product is introduced to the market. In a first look review, usually no comparison with competitive solutions is made, but features and benefits of the product are at the centre of the review.

2. Competitive reviews
    These reports are typically lengthy articles over several pages taking a very close look at all products competing in a certain market. Comparisons between all products are made based on different criteria.

3. Annual product awards
    Many publications run annual competitions to identify the best product of the year in a certain category. The election process can be very different from publication to publication. Some measure by market share, some measure by editor's choice, some measure by readers' choice.

Tests in the media can be either the result of the test lab purchasing the products anonymously in their local shop, or it is based on receiving test units from vendors.

Some vendors in fact run strong test unit programmes supporting the media not only with test units, but also with special support programmes.

These test unit programmes may not be considered to be part of classical PR. Nevertheless, they can be extremely important for the acceptance of the products by the public. Since they also address the media just like 'regular PR', we want to cover briefly aspects of measuring these programmes.

Needless to say it is impossible to influence a journalist or rather a test engineer, who you do not know. Tests done based on purchases made directly by the testing organisation should therefore not be covered here. The only recommendation that can be given in this context is that you should get to know testing institutions and media test labs well enough to check with them on a regular basis if they plan tests which may address some of your products. Based on this information you can take a reactive approach and try to make sure that your products are receiving a fair representation in the forthcoming reviews. In fact, here the aspect of relations in PR kicks in.

What can be measured well, though, is the result of a proactive test unit programme or awards programme you are running in your organisation.

A straightforward approach is to collect all test clips featuring your products and do some statistics on them, like counting how often your products won awards. Just as in 'regular' PR measurements, you should not just look at your own company's results, but do a comparison with the competition. It is a must to analyse competitive reviews and annual product awards. First look reviews of your products must be compared separately with respective reviews covering your competitors' products.

Compare apples with apples.

The next criterion to look at is what awards or ratings your products have actually won. Is it in categories like overall test winner, 'recommended by the editor', 'readers' choice' or best price/performance ratio? Is it always the same type of features that make you win, like performance, price, design or size, or is it different aspects that make you win different tests?

It is strongly recommended that you carry out a thorough analysis of awards, especially if you sell products to consumers. Here the number of tests and awards is extremely high across different publications and different countries. In the IT industry, for example, you can easily expect a product to participate in more than 100 product tests and reviews across Europe.

As an extension to the regular media analysis, Echo Research does a detailed qualitative and quantitative analysis of the awards data for Hewlett-Packard's Imaging and Printing Group on an on-going basis. Monthly reports show what competitive products are measured against your own products and what strengths and weaknesses become apparent from the test reports. A quarterly analysis then gives a good overview allowing you to identify trends.

An analysis of product reviews should be integrated into two closely related processes in your company:

1. The results of reviews are an extremely valuable source of information for the company's R&D department. Tests and reviews are a no-cost, unsolicited and independent source of information telling you how your products are perceived by users. These results should go directly into the planning of any future products.

2. In many countries winning awards in the media is so important that you want to promote these facts, either in additional PR (for example, press releases) or in advertising or in another way. You may want to promote it in flyers or direct mailings, you may want to promote awards in stores, you may want to have stickers on your products or on boxes. You obviously have many options – provided you have set up your organisation in a way that your marketing organisation and/or sales organisation gets automatic access to your media analysis – and provided that you were able to follow up with the publishing house which issued the award and get their permission to advertise with the awards and, for example, copyrighted logos that are involved.

Balanced Scorecard Template

Balanced Scorecard

Vision:

Strategy:

Field 1: Employees

Goal 1:

Measure 1:

Target value 1:

Tactic 1:

Goal 2:

Measure 2:

Target value 2:

Tactic 2:

Field 2: Processes

Goal 1:

Measure 1:

Target value 1:

Tactic 1:

Field 3: Customers

Field 4: Financials

List of Criteria for Measurements

In this chapter, we provide an overview of all criteria discussed in this book. For every criterion, we give a very brief reason for considering it ('+'), and we highlight some reasons – where applicable – why they may be of no value in certain situations ('–'), for example, because they may require too many resources.

INTERNAL MEASURES

Criteria	+/-	Comments	Page reference
Total number of interviews per time	+	Measures dedication of speakers.	17, 46
	-	Does not measure focus nor quality of interviews.	
Number of interviews per speaker	+	Internal incentive.	17, 46
	-	Does not measure quality of interviews.	
Number of press enquiries	+	Simple measure indicating interest of the media in your company.	16, 42
	-	It does not indicate the reason for the media's interest.	
Response times to press enquiries	+	Significant impact on PR performance.	14, 89
	-	Requires proper tracking.	
Number of hits on PR website	+	Measure indicating interest of the media in your company.	58
	-	It only provides limited information about the reason for the media's interest, if the visited pages are logged.	
Logistics at press conference	+	Allows measure of logistics agency, allows statements about impressions left with participants.	46
	-	Impact on PR results only indirect.	
Compliance with company's internal PR guidelines	+	Consistent internal processes result in consistent external appearance.	68
	-	In large corporations, in particular, internal processes can become serious inhibitors due to bureaucracy.	
Compliance with defined budget	+	Mandatory.	68
	-	N/A	
Updated PR website (virtual press room)	+	Note that nothing is as boring as a website that is not kept up to date!	69
	-	Requires additional resources.	
Updated journalist database	+	Allows news to be tailored to individual journalists' interests and needs.	68
	-	Could violate local legal demands on people's privacy.	
Updated contact/interview database	+	Allows future contacts to be tailored to skill level of individual journalist.	68
	-	Depending on the details tracked and the size of the organisation, this task could be very time consuming.	
Updated speaker database	+	Allows quick reactions to press enquiries.	68
	-	N/A	
PR training level of speakers	+	Good PR training enhances quality of interviews.	69
	-	N/A	
Presence of PR goals in business plan	+	Mandatory.	Chapter 2
	-	N/A	
Consistency across communication mix	+	Ensures maximum impact on the target audience.	22
	-	N/A	

QUANTITATIVE OUTPUT MEASURES

Criteria	+/-	Comments	Page reference
Clipping service	+	Commonly available service from a wide range of agencies.	1
	-	Easily leads to incorrect 'gut-feeling' based subjective conclusions. No quality measure, no comparison with competition.	
Total number of articles per time	+	Most simple volume measure, typical parameter delivered by basic media evaluation services.	10, 16, 26, 53, 57, 75
	-	No quality measure, no comparison with competition.	
Total number of articles per project (e.g. per press release distribution)	+	Basic volume measure for a PR project.	57
	-	No quality measure.	
Total number of articles per region per time	+	Allows basic volume comparison e.g. across countries.	65, 73
	-	No quality measure, does not take into account potentially different competitive position across countries.	
Total number of articles per topic or per product	+	Good basic measure for business executives or marketing managers per product range.	73
	-	Requires good briefing of research agency and exact definition of search keywords.	
Total number of articles per publication	+	Basic volume measure for receptiveness of publications. Comparison across publications with different publication cycles is not recommended.	75
	-		
Total number of articles per journalist	+	Basic volume measure for receptiveness of individual journalists, particularly interesting to measure output of freelance journalists.	53
	-	Does not cover journalists' attitude.	
'Impressions' (volume, taking into account circulations of publications)	+	Good and simple volume measure for the outreach of generated coverage.	57, 73, 97
	-	Difficult to measure for online publications, since circulation is not always available.	
'Impressions' taking into account multiple readers per copy OTS (opportunity to see)	+	Sophisticated volume measure for the outreach of generated coverage.	58, 98
	-	Difficult to measure for online publications, since circulation is not always available.	
Simple advertising equivalent	+	Volume measure for 'controlling focused management'.	59
	-	No quality measure, does not take into account different impact of press article and advertising.	
Advertising equivalent taking into account article favourability	+	Volume measure for 'controlling focused management'.	61
	-	Reliable parameters comparing impact of advertising and press articles are subjective.	
Corporate/brand/product tracking	+	Separates coverage for different internal stakeholders.	78
	-	N/A	

Criteria	+/-	Comments	Page reference
Volume growth rate	+	Shows trends over time.	16
	-	Does not show absolute values.	
Volume displayed as market share	+	Displays visibility of competitors.	75
	-	Does not show absolute values.	
Distribution by type of press	+	Shows if message matches target audience.	76
	-	Only relevant if mix of target audiences is addressed.	
Number of speaker references	+	Indicates attractiveness and effectiveness of company speaker.	78
	-	Does not reveal if the right messages were quoted.	
Number of headlines	+	Better indicator for visibility than just number of articles.	78
	-	Does not reveal if headline content is according to intended message.	
Number of articles per industry topic	+	Good indicator of what is a hot topic in the industry.	79
	-	Not company specific! This is only an indirect measure of your PR efforts.	
Calibrated volume	+	Takes into account company sizes.	78
	-	Could become complex if company contributes to different markets and is difficult to compare.	

QUALITATIVE OUTPUT MEASURES

Criteria	+/-	Comments	Page reference
Favourability rating by positive/neutral/negative	+	Easy indicator for quality of coverage and for the image of the company in the media.	63, 76
	-	Can be very subjective.	
Favourability rating on fine scale	+	Useful for index calculations.	63, 76
	-	Can be very subjective.	
Favourability rating vs. competition	+	Allows comparison across countries.	64, 65
	-	Does not consider company sizes (that is, 'PR power').	
'Slugging average'	+	Simple indicator for quality of coverage.	76
	-	Does not take the impact of an article into account.	
Prominence	+	Gives a good indication of the impact an article makes for a certain company.	77
	-	Could be subjective. You need to define prominence well before you measure it.	
Use of picture material	+	Adds a dimension to content understanding and recall.	62
	-	The wrong picture may be chosen by the journalist, thus the existence of picture material alone would not say anything about the quality.	
Analyst quotes	+	It makes the article look neutral and more independent.	39, 63, 78
	-	Negative quotes can be extremely damaging.	
Article placement in publication	+	It indicates the level of importance of the information for the readers as judged by the journalist. Important parameter, if the article is measured against advertising equivalent.	39
	-	Additional analysis cost.	
Headline text	+	It shows how the press prioritises your message.	39, 62
	-	Can be subjective.	
Comparison 'intended message vs. coverage'	+	Indicates the effectiveness of your company spokespeople	40
	-	Only works if the intended message has been clearly defined before the launch of the PR campaign.	
Spokespeople quotes	+	Gives more power to the article.	40, 63
	-	If wrong quote is chosen, it can mislead the reader.	
Article content meets readers' expectations	+	This measure closes the loop with the target audience. Indicates if your messaging was focused to the target audience.	40
	-	A sophisticated evaluation could be expensive and time consuming.	
Diagram 'volume over favourability rating'	+	Good overview especially when displayed against competition.	79
	-	Different criteria can be selected for volume and favourability giving different results.	
Demographics of reached audience	+	Good first indicator for results on outgrowth level.	64
	-	High cost/value ratio.	

CRITERIA TO MEASURE RELATIONSHIPS

Criteria	+/-	Comments	Page reference
Position in attitude/ perception grid	+	Indicates a journalist's interest in a subject and allows long-term development tracking.	49
	-	Requires critical mass to position a journalist in the grid.	
Response times to invitations	+	It indicates a journalist's interest in a subject and is simple to measure.	48
	-	Does not take into account reasons for potentially slow responses.	
Attendance at events and so on	+	Easy to measure.	48
	-	'Bums on seats' is not a strong measure in itself.	
Proactive requests for interviews and opinions	+	Strong indicator of interest in your company.	42
	-	The reason for the requested contact or interview can be positive or negative.	
Response to surveys	+	Good indicator of attitudes towards your company; 'open' questions preferred.	48
	-	Only of limited use if done anonymously.	
Publicly positive statements	+	Best to hope for in PR!	49
	-	Consider cultural aspects!	

CRITERIA TO MEASURE OUTGROWTH

Criteria	+/-	Comments	Page reference
Awareness and preference study	+ -	Very detailed and focused. Costs may only be justified for larger corporations.	85
Feedback, formal or informal	+ -	Easy to gather, reliability increases with sample size. Can be subjective.	48, 58
Test market analysis	+ -	Very precise. Time consuming.	60, 86
Target audience to recall PR campaign content	+ -	Gives a basic understanding of the impact at the outgrowth level. The evaluation is time and resource consuming.	26

CRITERIA TO MEASURE OUTCOME

Criteria	+/-	Comments	Page reference
Revenue development	+ -	The 'ultimate measure' for ROI (return on investment). Impact of PR can hardly be singled out.	4, 11, 60, 62
Comparison of awareness and preference studies	+ -	Reasonable cost, comparable over long periods. Difficult to single out impact of PR, especially of individual PR campaigns.	85
Comparison of pre-introduction tests	+ -	Very precise, impact of PR can be singled out. Too academic, time-consuming, expensive.	60, 86
Company reputation measure	+ -	Sophisticated, see, for example, Delahaye's MRi index (Appendix B). Recommended only for large corporations.	97
Specific pre- and after-campaign surveys	+ -	Detailed results. Expensive, questionnaire and execution critical.	65
Attitude change (attitude grid)	+ -	Good criterion if measured across a large sample. Can be subjective.	49
Postings on newsgroups and contributions to chat rooms	+ -	Direct access to opinions from your ultimate target group, your customers. Atypical and unrepresentative opinions are given in chat rooms.	86
Immunity to competitive messages	+ -	Best indication for proactive PR and for journalists' trust. Can be subjective.	86

Literature

1. *Publicity Power*, Charles Mallory, Crisp Publications, 1989 (German: PR-Power, Ueberreuter Verlag, ISBN 3 901260 92 7)

2. 'Evaluation von Public Relations' (Evaluation of Public Relations), Karin Kirchner, *pr magazin* 19/96

3. *GPRA-Empfehlungen zur Evaluation von Public Relations*, Gesellschaft Public Relations Agenturen e.V., May 1997

4. *Evaluation von Public Relations*, Dokumentation einer Fachtagung, Arbeitskreis Evaluation der GPRA, ISBN 3 927282 52 9, 1997

5. 'PR-Evaluation – Ein strategischer Faktor in der Kommunikationsarbeit' (PR evaluation – a strategic factor in communication), Argus Media GmbH, *Observer RTV*, November 1998

6. *Value-Added Public Relations*, Thomas L. Harris, NTC Business Books, 1998, ISBN 0 8442 3411 7 (hardcover), ISBN 0 8442 3412 5 (paperback)

7. *PR-Evaluation*, Petra Wochnik, Lehrveranstaltung Universität Hohenheim, 2. February 1999

8. *Public Relations on the Net*, Shel Holtz, Amacom, 1999, ISBN 0 8144 7987 1

9. *30 Minuten für erfolgreiche Presse- und Öffentlichkeitsarbeit*, Jens Ferber, 2000; Gabal Verlag, ISBN 3 89749 044 7

10. *Grundwissen Öffentlichkeitsarbeit*, Werner Faulstich, 2000, Wilhelm Fink Verlag

11. *Handbuch der Public Relations*, Albert Oeckl, Süddeutscher Verlag München, 1964

12. 'The Role of Rating in the PR activity', E. Bahareva, *Marketing*, 1, 2000, ISSN 1028 5849

13. 'The fall of advertising and the rise of PR', Al Ries and Laura Ries, *Harper Business*, 2002, ISBN 0 06 008198 8

14. 'The public relations research and evaluation toolkit', *PRCA, IPR, PR Week*, April 1999 (1st Edition)

15. *Primer of Public Relations Research*, Don W. Stacks, The Guildford Press, 2002, ISBN 1 57230 726 9

16. *Guidelines for measuring relationships in public relations*, Linda C. Hon and James E. Grunig, The Institute for Public Relations (available online at http://www.instituteforpr.com/measeval/rel_p1.htm)

17. *Public relations research for planning and evaluation*, Walter K. Lindenmann, The Institute for Public Relations, 2001

18. *Selling public relations research internally – changing the mindset about communications*, Lisa Richter and Walter G. Barlow, The Institute for Public Relations, 2001

Index

added value, PR 3–4
advertising
  credibility 60
  measurement problems 60
advertising equivalents (AVEs), and PR
    campaigns 59–62
agencies, PR
  evaluation criteria 32
  selection 31–3
  specialisation 30–31
American Chamber of Commerce 56
articles
  assessment criteria 39–40
  coverage level 78
  cultural issues 64
  headlines 39
  impression value 74
  influence tracker 61–2
  judgment on company 40
  number per publication 75–6
  placement in publication 39
  prominence 77
  quotes 40, 63
  rating scale 63
  size 39–40
  'slugging average' 76–7
  targeted messages 40
  tone 39, 76
  value measurement 61–2
attitude/perception measurement,
    journalists 49–51
audiences, target 22

balanced scorecard 23–4, 25
  template 102
brand tracking 78
budget, measurement 29–30
business fundamentals 14
  Hewlett-Packard 20
  internal measures 19
  large companies 21
  objective 15
  PR 16–21
  qualitative measures 19
  quantitative measures 19
business plan 21

calibrated volume, PR 78
CARMA International 84
CeBIT Fair (Hanover) 45, 46
communication plan, PR 22
company update 39–40
Compaq 67
competitors, comparison 11, 45, 82–3
coverage level
  articles 78
  industry topics 79
  press conferences 53–4
crisis situations
  anticipated 91
  examples 87–8
  external measurement 89
  internal measurement 89
  management 88
  measurement 89, 91
  predictable 89–90
  procedures 88
  unanticipated 92
cultural issues
  articles 64
  press conferences 49
customers 24–5

database
  contacts 68
  journalists 68
  spokespeople 68–9
Deutsche Telekom 2
direct marketing campaigns 22
Drucker, Peter F. 8

Echo Research 72
employees, PR 24
evaluation criteria, agencies 32
executives, media promotion of 37–8

Faulstich, Werner 11
favourability/circulation diagram 81–2
feedback questionnaire, journalists 95–6
finance 25

General Electric 21

About the authors

Dr Ralf Leinemann has more than 15 years' experience working in international PR, marketing and business development departments in the high-tech industry. He holds a PhD in Physics from the University of Tübingen, Germany. He joined Hewlett-Packard in 1989, initially in technical marketing for real-time computer systems. Afterwards, Leinemann did product marketing for workstations and industrial systems. He then did business development for technical systems with a focus on the telecom industry, before he moved into Public Relations. He started his career in PR as the PR manager for HP's computing systems in EMEA (Europe, Middle East and Africa). In that role he managed all external communication for that business in EMEA. He then integrated all communication for HP's business-to-business (B2B) solutions. He is currently the Communication Manager for Hewlett-Packard's Imaging and Printing Group in EMEA with a focus on the consumer space. In 2003, he was selected to appear in the *Who's Who of Professionals*.

Elena Baikaltseva has been Public Relations and Marketing Communications Manager for Advanced Micro Devices (AMD) in the representative office in Moscow since 2001. She has eight years' experience in communications functions, working for the international high-tech corporations Hewlett-Packard and AMD, and collaborating with PR agencies. Her responsibilities today include PR for AMD in Russia and the CIS countries with a strong focus on consumer markets. Elena Baikaltseva graduated from Institute Molodyezhi in 1995 and has a Higher Education Degree in Management and Administration. Since 1995 she has worked in Hewlett-Packard Company in various marketing and communication positions focusing primarily on enterprise market segments. She started her career in PR initially as PR manager for the HP Enterprise Computer Systems Organisation, a role which later developed into PR Professional for HP Russia, being responsible for planning, developing and execution of marketing communication and public relations programmes for all HP product categories. Elena Baikaltseva has vast experience in the management of integrated marketing campaigns and in the integration of international and regional PR projects of different scales.